The Christian Experience of Salvation

LAYMAN'S LIBRARY OF CHRISTIAN DOCTRINE

The Christian Experience of Salvation

WILLIAM E. HULL

BROADMAN PRESS
Nashville, Tennessee

© Copyright 1987 • Broadman Press

4216-39

ISBN: 0-8054-1639-0

Dewey Decimal Classification: 234

Subject Heading: SALVATION

Library of Congress Catalog Card Number: 84:20501

Printed in the United States of America

Unless otherwise noted, Scripture quotations are from the Revised Standard Version of the Bible, copyrighted 1946, 1952, © 1971, 1973.

Scripture quotations marked (KJV) are from the King James Version of the Bible.

Library of Congress Cataloging in Publication Data

Hull, William E.
  The Christian experience of salvation.

  (Layman's library of Christian doctrine; v. 9)
  Includes index.
  1. Salvation. I. Title. II. Series.
BT751.2.H85   1987   234   84-20501
ISBN 0-8054-1639-0

To
the memory of my parents

William Edward Hull
Margaret Jackson King Hull

In whose lives I first encountered
the Christian experience of salvation

Foreword

The *Layman's Library of Christian Doctrine* in sixteen volumes covers the major doctrines of the Christian faith.

To meet the needs of the lay reader, the *Library* is written in a popular style. Headings are used in each volume to help the reader understand which part of the doctrine is being dealt with. Technical terms, if necessary to the discussion, will be clearly defined.

The need for this series is evident. Christians need to have a theology of their own, not one handed to them by someone else. The *Library* is written to help readers evaluate and form their own beliefs based on the Bible and on clear and persuasive statements of historic Christian positions. The aim of the series is to help laymen hammer out their own personal theology.

The books range in size from 140 pages to 168 pages. Each volume deals with a major part of Christian doctrine. Although some overlap is unavoidable, each volume will stand on its own. A set of the sixteen-volume series will give a person a complete look at the major doctrines of the Christian church.

Each volume is personalized by its author. The author will show the vitality of Christian doctrines and their meaning for everyday life. Strong and fresh illustrations will hold the interest of the reader. At times the personal faith of the authors will be seen in illustrations from their own Christian pilgrimage.

Not all laymen are aware they are theologians. Many may believe they know nothing of theology. However, every person believes something. This series helps the layman to understand what he believes and to be able to be "prepared to make a defense to anyone who calls him to account for the hope that is in him" (1 Pet. 3:15, RSV).

Contents

1

The Process of Salvation

Christianity is, above all else, a religion of salvation. In the Old Testament, God alone "works salvation" (see Ex. 14:13) and indeed "is salvation" (see Ex. 15:2). He declared, "I, I am the Lord, and besides me there is no savior" (Isa. 43:11), leading the psalmist to exult: "God is our salvation. Our God is a God of salvation" (Ps. 68:19-20).[1] In the New Testament, Jesus defined His mission as coming "to seek and to save the lost" (Luke 19:10). This caused His followers to formulate a saying "sure and worthy of full acceptance, that Christ Jesus came into the world to save sinners" (1 Tim. 1:15). Our faith is synonymous with salvation more than with any other religious reality.

That being so, it is alarming to see how shriveled the concept of salvation has become in the understanding of many who claim to have experienced its impact in their lives. It is commonplace today to speak of "getting saved" as an isolated event affecting only the inner life of one individual at a climactic point in time, often in early childhood. This narrowing of the concept of salvation stands in glaring contradiction to its most basic biblical meaning. The earliest terminology used in the Old Testament for "to save" was based on a root meaning "to become roomy, broad, spacious" in contrast to the notion of "to be confined, constricted, oppressed."[2] In other words, deliverance was understood as rescuing a life which had been hemmed in on every hand by moving it out into the open. Ironically, we have allowed popular usage to restrict the very doctrine which calls us to enlarge our understanding.

Therefore, our first task in grasping the meaning of salvation is to gain a broader awareness of the scope of Christian deliverance. Since we shall be limiting our study to the human side of this experience, we may best begin by grasping the nature of salvation in all three of its tenses—past, present, and future—as they unfold in the life of each believer. Viewed in this way, salvation is seen not just as a point but also as a process, not just as a transaction but also as a development, not just as a status but also as a journey. Only as we move from static to dynamic concepts are we able to appreciate this doctrine in its biblical expression.

The Three Tenses of Salvation

True to its dynamic character, salvation appears in the New Testament primarily as a verb of action rather than as a noun of being. A look at its religious usages shows immediately, as J. B. Lightfoot put it, "Salvation is a thing of the past, a thing of the present, and a thing of the future."[3] That is, the tense of the various verb forms points to a fundamental distinction in the way that salvation is experienced. Let us examine a few biblical texts in each time category in order to illustrate these differences.

Salvation as Past

Especially in the later writings of the New Testament, such as Ephesians and the Pastoral Epistles, there are passages which view salvation as something already given and experienced in the past. For example, the familiar Ephesians 2:8 states that "by grace you *have been saved*," using the perfect tense to describe an accomplished fact with continuing results. In the Pastorals, the aorist tense anchors the saving act even more firmly in the past. Second Timothy 1:9 identifies God in His power as the one "who *saved* us," while Titus 3:5 similarly affirms that God our Savior in His mercy "*saved* us" (author's italics).

When we ask why these passages should locate salvation so exclusively in the past, it is because the saving work of Jesus Christ lies at a fixed historical period in the past. As 1 Timothy 1:15 puts it, "Christ Jesus *came* into the world to *save* sinners" (author's italics). The writer of Hebrews liked to stress that salvation originated with Jesus Christ who was its pioneer or trailblazer (2:10), its cause or source (5:9), its author or founder (12:2). Thus, one aspect of our salvation is inescapably located in the past because it is grounded in the unique, unrepeatable, once-for-all life, death, and resurrection of our Savior (Heb. 7:27; 9:12; 10:10). That being true, as soon as we begin to experience Christian salvation, we are dealing with something that is already completed. Our own experience is far from finished, but the reality on which it rests is in no way incomplete.

Salvation as Present

But the very same New Testament writers could speak with equal emphasis of salvation as a reality unfolding in the present. Paul, for example, in 1 Corinthians 1:18 described the word of the cross as the power of God to those who are now *"being saved"* (present tense), and later in the same book he identified his gospel which the Corinthians had earlier received as the message by which they are now "being *saved*" (present tense) if they continue to hold it fast (15:2). This challenge to steadfastness is repeated in Philippians 2:12, where Christians are to persist in working out their own salvation with fear and trembling; in Hebrews 2:3, where they are not to neglect the great salvation already confirmed to them; and in 1 Peter 2:2, where they are to leave spiritual infancy and grow up to the salvation which is theirs by eagerly desiring the pure spiritual milk of the gospel.

Reading only the traditional translation of the King James Version sometimes tends to obscure the force of the present tense in these and other passages. For example, in 2 Corinthians 2:15 the King James Version has: "For we are unto God a sweet savour of Christ, in them that *are saved*," as if their salvation were something already fully accomplished. But the original Greek text has a present participle which is best translated literally as "in the ones who *are now being saved*," with the implication that salvation is for them a not yet finished process. It is impossible to understand the spiritual imperatives of the New Testament without giving full weight to this present dimension. In dozens of ways its authors were saying: You have already been saved by the work of Christ on your behalf. Now, *become what you are* by experiencing this salvation as fully as possible in each moment of your ongoing lives!

Salvation as Future

Proof that salvation as understood by the New Testament is an open-ended pilgrimage is provided by those passages in which the reference is unmistakably future. Even though we emphasize this tense least, it is the most common category in New Testament usage. Paul said plainly in Romans 13:11, "Salvation is nearer to us now than when we first believed." Elsewhere he spoke of salvation as something yet to be "obtained" (see 1 Thess. 5:9; 2 Tim. 2:10), and Hebrews locates this final obtainment at the time of the second coming of Christ (9:28). That is what 1 Peter means by saying that Christians "are guarded through faith for a salvation ready to be revealed in the last time" (1:5) and that "as the outcome of your faith you obtain the salvation of your souls" (v. 9).

Whenever examples such as these are used to illustrate a particular point, the danger exists that the texts selected will be interpreted out of context. Therefore, we need to inquire whether the New Testament itself views salvation as occurring in three tenses within the same unified context. There are many passages which illustrate this interrelationship; for convenience I have selected two from Romans 5, providing a literal paraphrase designed to highlight the tenses used.

First, Romans 5:1-2 says, using various synonyms or "word pictures" for salvation: "Since we have already been justified (that is, acquitted)" in the *past*, "we now go on having peace with God" in the *present*, and, because of our current access to divine grace, we even now rejoice in the hope of one day "sharing the glory of God" in the *future*. Again, in verses 9-11, note the alternation of tenses: "Having already been justified by the blood (that is, death) of Christ" in the *past*, "we will one day be saved from wrath" by this same Christ in the *future*. "If God was willing to reconcile us to Himself through the death of His Son" in the *past* when we were still His enemies, "will He not even more be willing to save us" in the *future* since we now have Christ's life in us by faith? Being confident both of our reconciliation already received in the *past*, and of our salvation yet to come in the *future*, "we can now exult" in the *present* over what God *has* done, *is* doing, and *will* yet do for us through our Lord Jesus Christ!

Salvation in Three Stages

With the scriptural evidence before us, we are now ready to understand the doctrine of salvation in its three tenses. To simplify biblical usage, we may say that Christian salvation should always be viewed: (1) as a *past event*, uniquely focused on the saving ministry of Jesus Christ at the point where it first impinges on our lives; (2) as a *present experience*, the unfolding of the meaning of Christ's life for our ongoing lives; and (3) as a *future expectation* that the God who began a good work in us will bring it to completion at the day of Jesus Christ (Phil. 1:6). Thus salvation is to be viewed as a *point* in the past, as a *progression* in the present, and as a *perfection* in the future. It is from the first of these that we derive the idea of salvation as an instantaneous transaction; from the second of these as a lifetime of continuous training; and from the third of these as an eventual transformation. The key, of course, is to give balanced emphasis to all three of these tenses.

The Dynamic Experience of Salvation

With the biblical understanding of salvation firmly in place, we may now examine the experience itself in the light of its three tenses. The basic concept of salvation on which the Christian doctrine rests is the essence of simplicity. To be "saved," whether viewed physically or spiritually, describes an event with three parts: (1) We are saved *from* some peril. In ordinary life this might be from the fire that burns or from the water that drowns, but religiously we are saved primarily from sin. (2) We are saved *for* some purpose. In ordinary life this might be to fulfill our roles in the family, at work, or as a citizen; religiously, however, we are saved in order to achieve the full potential of our likeness to God. (3) Finally, we are saved *by* some person. In ordinary life the agent might be a bystander or friend, while the gospel declares that religiously we are saved by Christ. Let us now look at these three aspects in more detail.

The Peril from Which We Are Saved

Since sin is the great danger to which God responds in the offer of salvation, then how may we understand our deliverance in light of the three tenses clarified above?

(1) *We are saved from the penalty of sin in the past.*—None of us is born into a neutral environment, a spiritual vacuum. Instead, from the very beginning we are taught how to live by those whom sin has compromised. Our whole culture is organized around structures of prejudice that reinforce the influence of sin in our lives. Without help we are certain to succumb to the same temptations which enslaved both our forebears and our contemporaries. But in Christ we meet the one and only person who is different. He felt the full force of sin both in the compromises of His closest friends and in the social systems of His day, but never once did He yield to such pressures. Even though it cost Him His life to resist the full fury of evil, by so doing He broke its dominance over human life for the only time in history. At last sin had met its match, thus offering all who came after Him the option of overcoming the bitter legacy of Adam. By claiming the help of Christ, we may, for the first time, begin to battle sin without the certainty of defeat (compare Rom. 5:12-21).

(2) *We are saved from the power of sin in the present.*—When we try to cope with evil without the help of Christ, it always gains the upper hand, causing us to sin without conscience or constraint (Rom 1:18-32). Even our efforts to curb these ugly impulses with religious rules and regulations prove futile (Rom 2:1 to 3:20). But once the power of salvation begins to work in our lives, Christ gains the upper hand. Sin still lurks in the shadows as a beaten foe, but it no longer reigns over us in highhanded fashion as a tyrant would treat a slave (Rom. 6). To be sure, sin remains so close at hand that we still cannot keep all of the religious rules and regulations, but our anguished frustration over this failure is relieved by the certainty that Christ will win the final victory (Rom. 7). Therefore, because we are now free from divine condemnation for our failures, we can face every threat secure in the boundless love of God (Rom. 8). Sin is still present, but it is no longer able to prevail.

(3) *We are saved from the presence of sin in the future.*—To borrow a military metaphor, when Christ comes into our lives it is like "D day." A superior force has established a beachhead and the enemy has been put to flight. But the battle is not over. A "mopping-up operation" is required until "V-day" when every enemy weapon is silenced. For the Christian, that final triumph comes only after all of life has been lived, after all of God's creation has been redeemed, after every enemy has been subdued and the triumph of the risen Christ is complete (1 Cor. 15:20-28). When that happens, evil will be banished forever; and we shall at last enjoy the perfection known only to God.

The Purpose for Which We Are Saved

In daily life, an obvious danger demands our immediate attention regardless of who the victim might be. We would run to snatch a little child from in front of an onrushing automobile without pausing to evaluate how useful a life the wayward tyke might one day grow up to live. Because of this natural instinct to avert tragedy without first asking any questions, we tend in the religious area to think much more about what people are being saved *from* than about what they are being saved *for*. All of us have heard revival sermons designed to snatch people out of the flames of hell without ever suggesting the positive purpose of their deliverance. But the Bible is much more specific in defining the divine purpose for salvation and, as might be expected, each aspect clusters around one of its three tenses.

(1) *We are saved for an experience of grace in the past.*—No sooner are we rescued from the peril of sin than the realization begins to dawn that this was none of our doing. Instead, the whole act of deliverance was sheer gift precisely because we were completely helpless, slaves to the sin we willingly served. This recognition, both of our complete inability to save ourselves and of the high risk taken to snatch us from peril, leads to the description of this experience as *grace,* which means simply that salvation is utterly free. In our rebellion, we neither desired it nor deserved it, and when at last we accepted it there was nothing we could offer in return (compare Eph. 2:4-9; Titus 3:3-7). Once salvation is recognized as "amazing grace," then that insight provides a central clue to the character of God. Now all of life is seen as a vast givenness, lavish in its extravagance and limitless in the gratitude which it evokes from its astonished recipients.

(2) *We are saved for an experience of growth in the present.*—As a familiar hymn puts it, "Love so amazing, so divine, Demands my soul, my life, my all."[4] But gifts such as these cannot be given only once; instead, they must constantly be renewed amid the changing circumstances of life. The more we mature, the more we have to offer. Just as salvation is a continuous act of divine grace, so our response to it must be a continuous act of human gratitude. The New Testament leaves no doubt that what God wants most from us is steady growth toward that spiritual adulthood which Paul defined as "the measure of the stature of the fulness of Christ" (Eph. 4:13). To become ever more Christlike is the endless challenge of all who owe their very existence to the saving intervention of God in His Son.

(3) *We are saved for an experience of glory in the future.*—The more we grow in conformity to the image of God's Son (Rom. 8:29), the more we share the glory which is already His by His triumphant exaltation on high (2 Cor. 3:18). In 2 Timothy 2:10, Paul expressed a willingness to endure any hardship in his ministry "for the sake of the elect, that they may also obtain salvation in Christ Jesus *with its eternal glory*" (author's italics). Since glory is a supreme attribute of God Himself, what this incredible hope affirms is that we may look forward to an endless existence filled with the presence of God in all His greatness. As 2 Peter 1:4 puts it, our "precious and very great promises" are that one day we will "escape from the corruption that is in the world because of passion, an ' become partakers of the divine nature."

The Person by Whom We Are Saved

Between the plight *from* which we are saved and the purpose *for* which we are saved stands the person of Jesus Christ as the agent through whom this change is made possible. There is never a hint in the New Testament that we can be saved either by our own ingenuity or by the intercession of family and friends. Neither religion nor philosophy nor morality, valuable as they are, can break the stranglehold of sin and bring healing to a broken selfhood. Only Christ, who in His earthly life conquered sin, can restore a person to wholeness. Once again, this is seen in Scripture as happening in three stages.

(1) *We are saved by the incarnate Christ in the past.*—In taking unto Himself the totality of human existence (John 1:14), Jesus Christ became vulnerable to the full force of sin as we encounter it—that is, He was "one who in every respect has been tempted as we are" (Heb. 4:15). This testing reached a climax in Gethsemane as He faced the cross, but, at the price of infinite suffering, He refused to yield even for a moment (Mark 14:32-36). It was not that He was immune to our struggle; rather, by struggling more than any of us could ever imagine, "He learned obedience through what he suffered; and being made perfect he became the source of eternal salvation to all who obey him" (Heb. 5:8-9). Our salvation is not a theological proposition or a psychological mechanism. It is a historical achievement, a concrete victory that actually happened in time and space, a new thing that forever changed the possibilities available to the human race.

(2) *We are saved by the indwelling Christ in the present.*—But this fundamental alteration of reality achieved by Jesus Christ was not limited to the time and place in which it happened. His resurrection from the dead liberated His Spirit to live with His own in every time and place (that is, to the close of the age and the ends of the earth; compare Matt. 28:20). In terms of our experience, the Spirit "contemporizes" the salvation wrought by Christ in first century Palestine, making it relevant to each new situation which we encounter (compare John 16:7-15). Romans 8 is a magnificent exposition of the many ways in which the Spirit of Christ mediates the gifts of salvation to every believer: freedom (vv. 1-8), life (vv. 9-11), adoption (vv. 12-17), hope (vv. 18-25), intercession (vv. 26-27), purpose (vv. 28-30), and victory (vv. 31-39).

(3) *We are saved by the invincible Christ in the future.*—But even the many gifts of the Spirit do not exhaust the fullness of salvation. They are

but the "first fruits" of a vastly greater harvest (Rom. 8:23), the "down payment" or "earnest money" deposited to guarantee a much richer inheritance in the future (see 2 Cor. 1:22; Eph. 1:14). The role of the Holy Spirit is to remind us of what is yet to come as much as it is to remind us of what has already been. One day the Christ who came first in obscurity will come again in splendor to complete His saving work. The contrast between the two comings could not be greater: the first to be killed in shame on a cross, the second to be hailed as sovereign by every creature in the universe (Phil. 2:6-11). That day will also reveal an equally great contrast between our present and our future salvation. "Beloved, we are God's children *now;* it does not yet appear what we shall be, but we know that *when he appears* we shall be like him, for we shall see him as he is (1 John 3:2, author's italics; compare Phil. 3:20-21).

The findings of this chapter are aptly summarized in a story related by G. B. Caird of a time when the former Bishop of Durham was approached by a member of the Salvation Army with the question, "Are you saved?" To which the bishop replied that it depended on which tense his inquirer meant—past, present, or future. Caird paraphrased his answer as follows: "If you mean 'Did Christ die for me?', undoubtedly; if you mean 'Are my feet firmly set upon the highway of salvation?', I trust so; but if you mean 'Am I safe home in the blest kingdoms meek of joy and love?', certainly not."[5] The basis for our assurance of future salvation is the forgiveness of our sins and our continuing experience of God's work of grace in us.

In the chapters that follow, I trace the drama of salvation as it unfolds in human experience from beginning to end. In so doing, I ground this process in the saving work of Christ from the first act on earth to the final act in heaven. Please join me on this journey. It is the greatest pilgrimage on which any person may embark, for it is nothing less than the passage from darkness into light, from despair into joy, from death into life!

Notes

1. According to F. J. Taylor, "Save, Salvation," *A Theological Word Book of the Bible,* edited by Alan Richardson (New York: Macmillan, 1953), p. 219, "the phrase 'God saves' or 'God is salvation' (1 Sam. 14.39, 1 Chron. 16.35, Ps. 20.9, 68.20, Isa. 33.22) could almost be likened to a primitive creed."

2. Georg Fohrer, *Theological Dictionary of the New Testament*, edited by Gerhard Friedrich (Grand Rapids: William B. Eerdmans, 1971), vol. VII, p. 973.

3. Cited by A. M. Hunter, *Interpreting Paul's Gospel* (Philadelphia: Westminster, 1954), p. 22.

4. Isaac Watts, "When I Survey the Wondrous Cross," stanza 4.

5. G. B. Caird, *Principalities and Powers* (Oxford: Clarendon, 1956), pp. 80-81.

Bibliography

Bloesch, Donald G. *The Christian Life and Salvation*. Grand Rapids: William B. Eerdmans, 1967. 164 pages.

Conner, Walter T. *The Gospel of Redemption*. Nashville: Broadman Press, 1945. 369 pages.

Green, E. M. B. *The Meaning of Salvation*. Philadelphia: Westminster Press, 1965. 256 pages.

Hunter, Archibald M. *Interpreting Paul's Gospel*. Philadelphia: The Westminster Press, 1954. Pages 21-55.

Scott, Charles A. Anderson. *Christianity According to St Paul*. Cambridge: University Press, 1927. 284 pages.

Smith, C. Ryder. *The Biblical Doctrine of Salvation: A Study of the Atonement*. London: Epworth Press, 1941. 320 pages.

Stevens, George Barker. *The Christian Doctrine of Salvation*. The International Theological Library, edited by Charles A. Briggs and Stewart D. F. Salmond. New York: Charles Scribner's Sons, 1905. 546 pages.

Part I
The Choice

Since salvation is a new possibility created for every person by the life, death, and resurrection of Jesus Christ, then it is an option which has been before the human race for almost two thousand years. There is really nothing that we can add to or subtract from the offer. Salvation is a given: for the taking or the leaving, for the accepting or the rejecting, for the believing or the denying. Every time the "old, old story" is told again, it lives in our hearing. Even when we try to dismiss its appeal with a shrug, the invitation persists; others claim it—or are claimed by it—never to be the same again. We may not like the changes which it demands, or which it produces, but still it stands squarely across the pathway of human existence as the great alternative which causes every road we take to fork.

Precisely because salvation *is,* as a given beyond our control, our initial encounter with it involves a choice. Long before we decide which choice to make, we come to realize that a clear-cut choice is not only inevitable but also important. For you see, salvation is not only *given* out of the long ago but also is a *gift.* We come upon it as something proffered. By its very nature, salvation is more than a gift; it is a gift *for us.* If it were some achievement created as an end in itself, such as the accomplishments of the caesars, then we could admire it from afar. Or if it were intended for someone else, we could pass it by without a second thought. But because of its essential character as a *gift-for-us,* we must do something about it. Salvation always comes as gospel, which means that it always comes on an outstretched hand. The gift is proffered even before we can set the terms of the encounter, which means the next move is up to us.

A multitude of decisions in life are inescapable; many of them, quite trivial. The difference here is that the offer of salvation involves a radical reorientation of my life beginning in the very depths of my being. Therefore, the decision which I make regarding this possibility is utterly crucial. For if Christian salvation really is "the answer," then it is the answer to my life's ultimate questions. And if it is not "the answer," then what I put in its place is going to be ultimate, at least for me. Either way, my choice involves a decisive fork in the road. When facing the salvation issue, I am at the watershed of destiny. I may resent having so momentous a decision thrust upon me, quite possibly by surprise, but there is simply no way I can soften either its necessity or its fateful consequences.

In some Christian traditions, the place of choice in the doctrine of salvation is understood quite differently. Because salvation has been a "given" for so many centuries, it seems almost to be taken for granted. Since the church has long been its custodian and mediator, infants may be baptized based upon their parents' status rather than upon their own decision. To be sure, they are nurtured to affirm this relationship in later years, but care is taken to make this as natural and normal as possible so that their faith will rest on the great heritage of the centuries. Personal choice is not emphasized. In denominations where this theological emphasis prevails, we are not surprised to find many members with no conscious awareness of having ever chosen to accept the salvation offered in Christ.

The purpose of this book is not to criticize such an approach or even to enter into friendly dialogue with its advocates. My purpose is to explain why many Christians do continue to emphasize the centrality of personal decision in the salvation process. For one thing, such an emphasis reflects fidelity to a strong scriptural teaching, as I hope the next three chapters will show. For another, it corresponds to the religious need of a great majority of the human race. Acceptance of Christian salvation would clearly involve a drastic reordering of priorities. This could hardly be achieved without making a number of far-reaching commitments regarding the basic values of life. This would be true in the so-called "Christian" nations of North America and Europe, where most of the citizens are devoted to secular materialism. It would also be true in the Second and Third Worlds, where most of the citizens either have no religion or are nominal adherents of a traditional culture-religion. Finally, it is a false antithesis to contrast "organic" approaches to salvation which emphasize group oneness with "individualistic" approaches which emphasize lonely decision. In a healthy church environment, there is no reason a mature congregation cannot guide the new convert to make mature choices—and so have the best of both approaches!

Having defended the importance of self-determination in the experience of salvation, I would hasten to add that the decision-making process need not be especially dramatic in order to be effective. Depending on the temperament and circumstances of the individual, there may be a great deal of emotion or very little at all. The needed choices may be made with decisive suddenness or quite gradually over an extended period of time. For some the whole matter may be intensely subjective, introspective, and private; while for others it may be very objective, communal, and public. Some will cry; others will laugh. Some will be cautious; others, impulsive. Some will be resolute; others will waver. All of this is but commentary on the unpredictability of human personality, not on the fickleness of divine salvation. There is simply no prescribed *pattern* of religious experience by which we must be saved!

Taking the New Testament as our guide, however, we can find three fairly predictable stages through which life passes in its awakening to the claims of God. We may view them as basic steps in the opening of selfhood to receive the salvation offered in the gospel. While the sequence does not always follow a prescribed order, the normal progression is to move from (1) repentance to (2) faith to (3) confession. In one sense, all three are ways in which we turn from a life that is being lost to a life that is being saved. In the next three chapters, we shall look at each of these components in the process of choice, asking what they mean and what they contribute to our experience of salvation.

2
Repentance

My wife and I were married on a hot summer afternoon in the east central Alabama community where her family had lived for generations. After finishing the reception, changing clothes, and bidding farewell, we were driven to our "getaway" car that we thought had been hidden from prying eyes, only to discover that pranksters had painted "Just Married" signs all over the exterior with white shoe polish and had tied a number of empty oil cans to the back bumper with clothes-hanger wire to call attention to their art work. Even though it was already dusk, there was nothing to do but return to the house, locate a pair of pliers, get down on all fours in my best "going away" outfit, and remove those clanging cans. This task, of course, left me covered with dirt and grease. By the time I had thoroughly scrubbed and driven away for the second time, it was almost dark.

As we started up the road, I discovered that in our haste to leave I had failed to pick up my recently acquired wedding band which I had removed temporarily while battling grime at the washstand. My bride quickly informed me that she was not about to leave on a trip with a man who did not have a wedding ring, so there was nothing to do but return, retrieve my badge of legitimacy, and set out for the third time on the back-country road that would take us to the Bankhead Highway (U.S. 78) in Heflin, Alabama, and thence to our overnight destination in Atlanta, Georgia. I tell you all of this to explain that it was thoroughly dark and we were hours behind schedule when finally we reached the courthouse square in the county seat town and began searching for roadside signs pointing to U.S. 78. As soon as we spotted the right highway number we set out in earnest, hoping to make up for lost time and to redeem an evening that had begun as a comedy of errors.

Apprehension began to mount, however, when I failed to reach the Georgia state line only about twenty miles east of Heflin. My worst fears were confirmed when we reached our first town and saw a sign indicating how many miles it was, not to Atlanta, but to Birmingham. We were on exactly the right road but were going in exactly the wrong direction! There was nothing to do but turn around and head back east rather than west, retracing twenty-five or thirty miles which represented further wasted time and effort. But at least we now knew that we were heading in the right direction, and, with that clarification, the rest of our honeymoon trip unfolded without mishap.

I have shared this experience with you because it provided me with an indelible impression of what repentance means: a turning around of life from going in the wrong direction to going in the right direction. I want to reflect upon our wedding trip as this chapter unfolds in the hope that it will offer you insight regarding a crucial component of the salvation experience that we seldom consider today because it has been distorted by connotations which are not scriptural.

The word *repentance* as used in both Old and New Testaments means basically a "turning to God." Relating the nature of such an act to the time categories clarified in the previous chapter gives us three aspects to the concept: (1) a turning *from* a wrong direction chosen in the *past;* (2) a turning *toward* a right direction chosen for the *future;* (3) a turning *around* so as to change directions in the *present.* Let us now examine each of these dimensions in more detail.

Repentance as a Turning from the Past

Back to that honeymoon itinerary for a moment. As we left Heflin, we were on a perfectly good road, smooth and wide and straight—in fact, the best road in Alabama before the interstate system began to be built. Furthermore, it was the *right* road, U.S. 78, not some detour or side road leading nowhere. There were many other motorists traveling with us in the same direction. I was obeying every traffic law, my automobile was functioning properly, and I was enjoying a delightful conversation with my beautiful bride seated beside me. We were on an important trip and seemed to be making good progress. A self-evaluation at that moment would have yielded a very favorable verdict. But despite all of those positive feelings there was one fatal flaw: By continuing as we were going, we would never reach our destination! Although everything seemed to be fine, unless there were a fundamental change of direction, we would utterly fail to fulfill our honeymoon plans.

The spiritual counterpart to that situation provides a starting point for our understanding of repentance. In setting the course of life, most people choose a well-traveled road that seems to offer many advantages. Our intentions are good. We are not bothering anybody else. We work hard and appear to be making reasonable headway. Our eventual goals are exciting, and we long for the day when they will be attained. But after a time, we fail to reach some of our anticipated milestones. Telltale signs along the way begin to suggest that merely to continue more of the same year after year will not get us where we want to go. Then we see some sign indicating plainly that we are headed in the wrong direction, that "more of the same" will actually make the problem worse! This disturbing disclosure may come through a personal crisis, a probing sermon, or a gentle hint from a friend. The suspicion can no longer be suppressed that, without some remedial action, we are never going to reach our intended destination.

Repentance begins with the recognition that life is moving in the wrong direction—no matter how long we have been doing it, no matter how many others may be doing the same thing, no matter how contented we are with our situation. Which says something significant about the seductiveness of sin. Evil is not always the flagrant violation of some moral code that sears the conscience and shames us in front of other people. Instead, it may be, as one biblical word picture describes it, just a missing of the mark, a straying from the path, a drifting toward the shoals.[1] For the moment, all seems to be going well. Only when we take a longer look and ask where all of this will lead do we realize that, without a drastic course correction, we will veer farther and farther from our goals.

Because sin is often defined in scandalous fashion, we tend to assume that repentance is "godly sorrow" in the sense of deep contrition for some outrage that has left us utterly mortified. That may be very true in some instances. But the mourner's-bench approach to repentance fails to touch the multitude of decent folk leading respectable lives who feel no need to pour out a tale of woe over a past of profligate degradation. Such people need to see that repentance is not limited to remorse over tragic blunders. It also involves the willingness to take a longer look, to analyze where life is really heading, and to redirect its thrust even when things seem to be going fairly well. Repentance speaks to an urgent need which we all feel, even if our past is not particularly sordid, to reorient life so that it will be centered around ultimate goals.

Think for a moment about the underlying sources of dissatisfaction in our lives. Most of us are not concerned primarily about our occasional lapses of conduct, regrettable as they may be, but about whether our marriages and our children and our jobs are really going anywhere. We have all known people whose marriages drifted into mediocrity, whose children were allowed to wander into aimlessness, whose jobs gradually lost their meaning and purpose. It all happened so slowly that the victim never really realized when a wrong turn had been taken. And that is our fear, that one day we will fail to reach our objective without ever really knowing where we went astray. Most of us miss the prize in life (Phil. 3:14), not because of some monstrous defiance of God, but because we live from day to day without ever really asking where it all will lead.

It is precisely to deal with the problem of ending up at the wrong destination that the imperative of repentance is designed. To repent does not mean to admit that you have done something worse than anybody else. Rather, it means to step back and take stock, to evaluate the present direction of life, and then to decide if you are pressing toward the best eventual outcome. To be sure, you may be so chagrined by this self-examination that it will bring searing grief. But the overriding mood should be one of joy that you have at last discovered your mistake and thus can do something about it. In such a moment of discovery, the need is not just for an emotional catharsis to end a guilt trip but for clear-headed commitments that point life in a different direction.

How may we make such commitments? Partly, of course, by a clear understanding of the nature of repentance, but primarily by a compelling attraction to the better option that awaits us if we will turn in a new direction. As long as we focus on our mistakes we are going to be unduly immobilized by guilt. Only as we turn from our present course and look in a new direction will we discover an alternative compelling enough to call us away from our wistful regrets. Let us look now at what this second stage in repentance involves.

Repentance as a Turning Toward the Future

Reflect with me once again on my honeymoon trip mishap. After realizing that we were headed in the wrong direction, I was surely the most exasperated driver in the state of Alabama. I could have stopped and rebuked myself for stupidity. I could have blamed my bride for not reading the road map better. I could have accused the Highway Department of not making the road signs clearer. But none of this finger pointing would have done any good. Instead of fussing at myself or my wife or the world in general, what I needed was simply to turn around and travel in the opposite direction. Something better awaited us in the opposite direction, and it was precisely that sense of "something better" that made us turn around as soon as possible.

The point is already obvious. Many people never get around to repenting either because they are too busy looking for somebody to blame for their situation or because they are already so set in their ways that they are willing to settle for second best. One thing is needed to overcome both obstacles: the assurance that a finer destination awaits them in the future if only they will abandon the way that they have been going in the past. This was exactly the strategy of Jesus as He began His ministry in ancient Galilee. Mark 1:15 summarizes Jesus' message as follows: "The time is fulfilled, and the kingdom of God is at hand; *repent,* and believe in the gospel" (author's italics). We might paraphrase that proclamation as follows: "One major period in human history is now drawing to a close and a new era is about to begin in which you will have the chance to live in anticipation of experiencing the long-awaited reign of God. Because this option is infinitely better than living under the limitations of the ancient law of Moses, I urge you to accept this finer alternative by relinquishing the status quo and embracing my good news with all your hearts."

Notice the implications of this pivotal passage. Jesus did not say that the kingdom of God had already arrived, only that it was near at hand. In other words, it was not present as something to be grasped but lay out in the immediate future as something to be avidly sought. We may illustrate by comparing the situation to sunrise. The kingdom, like the sun, had not yet risen, but its appearance was so imminent that the glow already filled the horizon. In that sense, repentance mean turning from darkness to dawn and journeying in hope toward the coming of the light (compare Acts 26:18). And why should the hearers of Jesus make so drastic a change? Because that reign of God foreshadowed by His message represented the fulfillment of every desire for which the children of Israel had been yearning for centuries. Jesus did not say, "Repent because you have done something terrible!" Rather, He said, "Repent, because God is about to do something wonderful!"

This announcement still strikes a responsive chord in our hearts. We have not only a vague dissatisfaction with the way things are going but also a yearning for "something better" in life. Fundamental to our human capacity for repentance is a heartache for significance, a longing for fulfillment, what Gordon Allport called "the appetite for meaning."[2] Simply put, we are never quite content with ourselves. That is why we read the biographies of great persons and dream about becoming like our heroes and make a string of New Year's resolutions and send off for courses in self-improvement. *All of us want a future that is better than our past!* Hence, the possibility of one day entering the kingdom of God, if that is really a viable option, offers an inducement to break with the past and redirect our lives, that is, to repent.

Unfortunately, for hundreds of years the notion of repentance has been entwined with the medieval Catholic doctrine of *penance,* which is the basis for a widespread misunderstanding—lamentably exploited by some clergy—that the heart of this experience involves "paying for" our follies by suffering the punishment of guilt. To be sure, sin does bring its own judgement into human life, but repentance itself is a glad turning from that oppressive burden of condemnation in the confidence that something better is about to come. The mood of the experience is one of expectancy, of anticipation, of rejoicing. The about-face should be a moment bursting with hope, for nothing so revolutionizes life as to be offered an alternative future. It awakens everything noble in the human spirit. That is why Henry Ward Beecher said, "Repentance is another name for aspiration."[3]

This mood of eager longing distinguishes Christian repentance from contemporary secular despair. In the modern period, existentialism has subjected the human condition to remorseless self-examination. The atheistic branch of this philosophy soon concluded that humanity is, indeed, going in the wrong direction, that meaninglessness or nothingness is sure to be its final destination. Thinkers such as Albert Camus and Jean Paul Sartre have written eloquently about the anguished despair that is the only honest attitude toward this grim prospect. Thus, if we as Christians view repentance only as pious breast-beating, as an orgy of self-accusation, we will find that this doctrine has little to offer our secular counterparts who have already pushed that theme to its limits. What humanity needs to hear in our doctrine of repentance is that there is a better option, that the future can be different from the past, that God is on the verge of doing a new thing in which we may each participate.

Repentance as a Turning Around in the Present

Once repentance is heard as good news rather than as bad news, then the true choice to be faced is whether one will accept this surprising option and thereby change direction even if others continue on as before. Such change is never easy. The situation is somewhat like the circus act when the trapeze artist lets go of one swinging bar and turns in mid-air to reach for another. That heart-stopping twist far above the crowds is risky business, but taking such a leap is what repentance is all about. John McCall once described it as "giving up what you have—which is safe, secure and certain—for what you don't have—which is unsafe, insecure and uncertain."[4] This means that the crux of repentance is the courage to choose, the willingness to take destiny into one's own hands, the daring to decide which future one will finally possess.

At least four formidable barriers stand across this momentous U-turn in life. One is the pride which makes us unwilling to admit that life has strayed off course. Another is the cynicism that ridicules the possibility of a better future because, being future, it has not yet been seen. A third is the skepticism that makes us wary of our ability to change because the force of habit enslaves us to predictable routine. A fourth is the fear that causes us to take self-protective measures against a future that is unknown and, therefore, dangerous. Assuming that we want to strike out in a new direction, what power is great enough to help us overcome all four of these obstacles to repentance?

In the Bible, encouragement to repent comes from an incredible quarter—God Himself! In almost forty Old Testament passages, God is said to repent, obviously not in the sense of renouncing His sins, for He is not man (Num. 23:19; 1 Sam. 15:29), but in the sense of His willingness to make a fresh start, to try again, to withhold judgment (Ex. 32:14; Jer. 26:13; Ps. 106:45). God is bound to His promises (that is, to the future, not to the past). He is not "a prisoner of His eternal immutability."[5] The supreme instance of this divine openness to a fresh initiative was seen in the sending of Christ when we least expected Him. In an ultimate sense, God turned to us in Christ so that in that same Christ we might turn to Him.

The profound implications of this truth are summarized in the claim of Jesus: "I have . . . *come* to *call* . . . sinners to *repentance*" (Luke 5:32, author's italics). The text clearly implies that repentance is not a work of our own doing but is a gift of Christ's coming and of His calling (compare Acts 5:31; 11:18). The parables of Luke 15 underscore that repentance is not so much a task which we complete as it is a response called forth by the offer of grace. Sinners repent (Luke 15:7,10) because they have first been rescued by a merciful initiative lying outside themselves:

by a shepherd who finds his sheep, by a woman who finds her coins, by a father who finds his son. When Jesus called His hearers to "repent" because "the kingdom of God is at hand" (Mark 1:15), He did not then say, "Go find a way to do this on your own." Rather, He moved immediately to *call* them to himself with the words, "Follow me" (v. 17), thereby indicating that He would personally lead them through the process of repentance as members of His disciple band.

Behind this strategy of Jesus lay the realization that life in the new world of the kingdom would require a totally new mind-set. Therefore Jesus did not simply order an about-face and then leave the people to march off as they pleased. Instead, He patiently taught them a whole new way to look at life, a fresh angle of vision on a whole range of vital issues. In fact, when the Old Testament word for *repentance,* which in its Hebrew form *(shub)* meant "turning" in the sense of "returning to God," came to be used in the New Testament, the Greek equivalent chosen *(metanoia)* meant "change of mind" in the sense of a metamorphosis of consciousness. By relating the two terms, what the Bible suggests is that we will never complete life's great turnaround unless we gain an entirely new perspective, a whole new way of thinking about the possibilities of the future.

We are now ready to answer the question of just how the gospel enables us truly to repent. Clearly the decision to stop going in one direction and to start going in another is our responsibility, but the incentive to make such a reversal is of God. Christ comes to us before we ever seek Him and offers a new option before we are even aware of what we are missing. He is so utterly free of the status quo, so remarkably open to the future, that His own life stands as the perfect incarnation of the meaning of repentance. With that boundless sense of freedom, He seeks us out in our lostness (Luke 15:1-2). He identified with us so deeply that, at last on the cross, He repented with us and for us even as He "calls" us to the same repentance.[6] Thus His insistence on repentance is both a gift and a demand, both an indicative in His life and an imperative in ours.

Central to repentance, then, both for Christ and for us, is the conviction that human nature can be changed, beginning at the very core of consciousness. The apostle Paul once entreated his readers to "be transformed by the renewal of your mind" (Rom. 12:2), which reflected His confidence that true repentance is the beginning of a renovation of our very existence. If only the *mind-set* can be radically reoriented, then the most profound consequences for thought, feeling, and volition will follow. And how may this happen? Elsewhere Paul appealed, "Let this *mind* be in you which was *also in Christ Jesus* (Phil. 2:5, KJV, author's italics). Which means that Christ's call to repentance is ultimately an offer to *give us His mind,* to replace our tired, old thought patterns with His revolutionary vision of the kingdom of God. Here we have it: Repentance is a "change of mind" that comes by exchanging our mind-set for the mind of Christ which He will freely give us as we respond to His call.

Notes

1. One word usually translated as *sin* in both the Old Testament *(hattath)* and the New Testament *(hamartia)* comes from a root meaning "to miss the mark." It may refer literally to the failure of an arrow to reach its target or of a traveler to take the right road to his destination. It may refer figuratively to the failure to fulfill one's duties or to reach one's goals. Evil in this sense is an erring, a deviation, a bent oriented away from God.

2. Cited and discussed by Emilie Griffin, *Turning: Reflections on the Experience of Conversion* (Garden City, N.Y.: Doubleday & Company, 1980), p. 32.

3. Carroll E. Simcox, compiler, *A Treasury of Quotations on Christian Themes* (New York: Seabury Press, 1975), p. 206, #2513.

4. Cited by Griffin, p. 132, as an elaboration of John Henry Newman: "If faith is the essence of the Christian life, it follows that our duty lies in risking upon God's word what we have for what we have not, and in doing so in a noble and generous way."

5. J.-Ph. Ramseyer, "Repentance," *A Companion to the Bible,* edited by J.-J. Von Allmen (New York: Oxford University Press, 1958), p. 359.

6. This is an emphasis in the writings of Karl Barth, effectively summarized by his translator, G. W. Bromiley, "Conversion," *The International Standard Bible Encyclopedia,* revised edition edited by Geoffrey W. Bromiley (Grand Rapids: Wm. B. Eerdmans Publishing Company, 1979), 1, pp. 769-770.

Bibliography

Barclay, William. *Turning to God: A Study of Conversion in the Book of Acts and Today.* London: Epworth Press, 1963. 103 pages. Reprint: Grand Rapids: Baker Book House, 1972. 103 pages.

Barth, Karl. *Church Dogmatics.* Volume IV: *The Doctrine of Reconciliation, Part 2.* Edited by G. W. Bromiley and T. F. Torrance. Edinburgh: T. & T. Clark, 1958. Pages 553-584.

Chamberlain, William Douglas. *The Meaning of Repentance.* Philadelphia: Westminster Press, 1943. 239 pages.

Griffin, Emilie. *Turning: Reflections on the Experience of Conversion.* Garden City, N.Y.: Doubleday, 1980. 189 pages.

3
Faith

Have you ever realized how the word *faith* has been made synonymous with the substance of the Christian religion? We speak quite naturally of "the Christian faith," but other world religions do not describe themselves in that fashion, such as "the Buddhist faith" or "the Hindu faith" or even "the Jewish faith." In fact, faith is not a major doctrine in most religions. But faith is so uniquely central to Christianity that it may properly define Christianity's essence. Why the difference? Because Christianity is fundamentally not an ideology or a heritage or a culture but a *relationship*, and faith is the name given to that development by which a person is united to Jesus Christ in a saving relationship.

In the previous chapter, we learned that repentance is the radical reorientation of mind-set by which we turn life in the right direction. Now we are ready to understand why the New Testament links repentance so closely with faith (for example, Acts 20:21). Once we begin to journey toward the fulfillment of life promised by the approaching kingdom of God, we do so with a companion every step of the way. Jesus Christ not only guides us to make a basic course correction in the heading of our lives but also gives us a personally escorted tour of that new horizon toward which we are pointed by His call.

Since repentance is the process by which we turn life in a new direction, then *faith is the process by which we fill life with a new relationship*. This suggests that we may best understand the stages of faith by comparing them to the steps we take in forming effective human relationships. Modern psychology has studied human relationships in detail. We are reassured when we discover how well our insights regarding the dynamics of relationships correlate with New Testament descriptions of saving faith. At least three distinct stages seem to be involved in forging ties between two persons: (1) Persons gain *confidence* that a stranger is worth meeting due to the efforts of someone who knows them both and

33

bears testimony that the contact would be beneficial; (2) persons make a *commitment* to experience together the unfolding of life in a covenant of loyalty and trust; (3) persons achieve *communion* through a mutual sharing so intense that it results in a virtual identity of being.

Even so brief a summary suggests that the sequence in these three steps is climactic. This same progression is reflected in the way that the New Testament uses the verb "to believe." The verb is used frequently in a variety of contexts. A rigid consistency is not possible, but the following pattern is discernable. In the Gospel of John, for example: (1) one gains confidence by *"believing that"* the claims of Christ are credible (see 20:31a); (2) on that basis, one makes a commitment by *"believing in"* Christ in the sense of relying on Him in each new situation (see 14:1); (3) out of the communion that results from placing life in His hands comes *"believing"* in the absolute sense of an identification with Christ as an end in Himself (see 4:53; 20:31b).

As in the case of repentance, each step in the process of faith is related to one of the three tenses so crucial to our experience of salvation: (1) believing that what the gospel declares about Christ is trustworthy is based primarily on the testimony of witnesses *in the past;* (2) believing in Christ as the one on whom I rely is essentially an affirmation that He can be trusted *in the future;* (3) believing Christ Himself in terms of direct encounter is fundamentally an effort to engage His spirit with my spirit *in the present.*

Let us now examine these three stages of faith in terms of their distinguishing characteristics. We shall look, first, at faith as confidence in the reports of Christ in the past. Second, we shall look at faith as commitment to the reliability of Christ in the future. And third, we shall look at faith as a communion with the reality of Christ in the present. In so doing, we shall view each stage as a separate aspect of one unitary experience. We shall see the gradual unfolding of a bonding process that links us for all time and eternity to Jesus Christ as Savior and Lord.

Faith as Confidence in the Reports of Christ

The normal way two people get acquainted is to be introduced to each other. Chance encounters may take place, but initial contact usually involves a third party who knows them both. In order to awaken interest in establishing a new relationship, this go-between may suggest ways in which two persons who have heretofore been strangers would find each other attractive. Even though it may take some urging by the mediator, once a sense of potential is established that the relationship could prove significant, then we are usually willing for the meeting to be arranged.

As involves Jesus Christ, this preliminary stage is set by the witness of believers to the gospel. We often think of such activity in terms of the formal preaching of evangelistic sermons, but it may just as well take place through the simple testimony of one layperson to another. In either case, Christian witnessing is essentially a ministry of introduction by which those who already know Christ interpret His significance to those who do not. To "preach . . . Christ" (2 Cor. 4:5) is to offer Him to others as a stranger to be met, a friend to be known, a relationship to be established. That is why Paul said, "Faith comes from what is heard, and what is heard comes by the preaching of Christ" (Rom. 10:17).

The dynamics of being introduced shift a bit, however, when the other person is a famous celebrity whom many people are eager to know, such as politicians who are influential or artists who are talented or movie stars who are beautiful. Now the issue becomes one of whether such an important person would like to know someone of lesser reputation. In other words, getting acquainted raises in acute form the question of status. Do I have as much to give this relationship as I am likely to receive? Even on a minor scale, we often shrink back as unworthy of involvement with those whom we consider our superiors for fear we will not be able to contribute our fair share to the interchange. Think, for example, of how many relationships you have avoided with people smarter than you because they might show you up in conversation, or with people wealthier than you because they might want to do something together which you could not afford.

Then what about meeting Jesus Christ? After all, He is surely the most famous person who ever lived. His wisdom and courage and goodness are so far beyond ours that we could never even remotely match them. The gospel declares Him to be the Lord of the universe, whereas we are insignificant creatures of time and space. Since the story they tell about Him is true, then He has everything to offer us; and we have nothing to offer Him. Could any introduction be more one-sided and unpromising? And yet the highest witness of those who already know Him is that He does, indeed, want to know each of us, regardless of our condition. In fact, the gospel dares to assert that He loved us even before we felt the slightest interest in loving Him (Rom. 5:8). Therefore, we may prepare to meet Him in the confidence that we will be more than welcome.

What I have tried to clarify to this point is that faith arises when we are introduced to Jesus Christ by those who already know Him. If the witnesses had not been changed by their own relationship to Christ, they would not have bothered to tell others about it. That is why Paul described the process as being "*from* faith *to* faith" (Rom. 1:17, KJV, author's italics). Before we are ever asked to believe in Christ, we are given the cumulative testimony of those who have believed in Him since the days of His flesh (compare 1 Thess. 2:13). That means our faith begins as something objective, a given outside our experience, a story to be believed because it has already been validated by those who tell it.

People have been presenting Jesus Christ to others for almost two thousand years. This very claim has been challenged by scoffers, threatened by persecutors, ignored by skeptics, and yet the living chain of testimony has never been broken. In one sense, we are asked to believe the most believable story ever told. After all, what other claim has been scrutinized so constantly for so many centuries? There are many today, as in every age, who reject the gospel of Jesus Christ as spurious, but the reasons for their rejection are not serious enough to undermine its veracity. The amazing power of the gospel to survive every attack is triumphant evidence of its legitimacy in each new era.

From this perspective, we grasp the first dimension of faith as "assent to" or "creedance in" the truth of the gospel. We begin by "believing that" the testimony of the church to her Lord is trustworthy and, therefore, that the doctrines of the Christian faith are reliable. Stated in more personal terms, this means that Jesus Christ really is the kind of person believers say He is, hence we need not fear that His reputation will be shaken in a few years as with so many world-famous celebrities who fade away and are quickly forgotten. Without this conviction that the claims made for Christ are credible, we would be reluctant to move forward in our relationship for fear of being deceived. But once the identity and integrity of Christ are assured, then we are in a position to confirm the objective witness of others with our own subjective experience. How may this be done?

Faith as Commitment to the Reliability of Christ

As just defined, the first stage in faith is a willingness to hear the gospel, to listen to the witness of those who have already entered into a saving relationship with Jesus Christ. In one sense, at this level we are "looking Christ over," considering His claims, becoming familiar with His person and work, deciding whether we want our relationship to be more than that of casual acquaintance. Now we reach a crucial second stage where our decision involves whether to go it alone or live life with Christ, whether to choose a self-centered or a Christ-centered existence. There is simply no way to enter into a meaningful relationship with other persons except by making room for them within our lives. At this stage, we must decide both how much room we want to make for Christ within our own houses of being and how deeply we want to get involved in His life as it continues to be lived out in the lives of His own (Matt. 25:40).

In making such a choice, we will be guided to a great extent by whether life for us is primarily thing-centered or person-centered (that is, whether reality is ultimately an It or a Thou). In the former option, life becomes functional and persons become means to an end; in the latter option, life becomes relational and persons become ends in themselves. All of us can see the profound significance of marital relationship with a spouse, learning relationship with a teacher, supportive relationship with a friend. Then why not risk a saving relationship with Jesus Christ in the light of what He has meant to so many persons for almost two thousand years? Are there not more potentialities to a lifetime of dynamic interaction with Him than with any other person who ever lived?

If we decide to enter into a personal relationship with Jesus Christ, how may this be done? Any time two people want to know each other better, they must bring genuine openness to the encounter. A mutual receptivity is essential in order to lower barriers imposed by strangeness. Deep realism is required if each is to know how the other truly thinks and feels and hopes. Nothing thwarts progress like showing only the "best side" by "putting up a front." The impelling desire is for authentic encounter, for knowing the real person, for being present to the other and truly hearing what each is trying to say. The trust level begins to rise when both feel that each truly understands the other. This breakthrough may involve a painful shattering of illusions, because sham and pretense need to be put aside if mutual confidence is to flourish. All of this takes a great deal of time and requires the uncoerced initiative of both parties to be successful.

These same dynamics are activated in forming an effective relationship with Jesus Christ. What we call *grace* refers to the openness of God to be known and loved which He demonstrated by giving Himself freely and unconditionally in His Son. Likewise, what we call *faith* refers to our openness to this divine initiative which we demonstrate by accepting

Christ freely and unconditionally into our lives. We invite God to share our human existence because He has first invited us to share His divine existence. The outgoing of God to us is grace, the outgoing of us to God is faith. Since it always takes two to form any relationship, grace and faith are inseparable in the divine-human encounter. (Eph. 2:8).

Because of this connection, faith is not so much a requirement or task (Eph. 2:9) as it is a readiness, a willingness, an availability to be known and loved. The deepest relationships are never earned by effort but result from mutual sharing that is spontaneous and uncontrived. As a relationship-building venture, faith is not limited either to activity or to passivity but is involved in the interaction of both. Faith is both a knowing and a being known, both a loving and a being loved, both a trusting and a being trusted. It is both the activity of "letting go" and the passivity of "letting God." When we enter into authentic relationships with other persons, we neither control them nor are we controlled by them. That is why from one perspective faith may be seen as complete freedom but from another perspective as complete submission.

Perhaps the best word to describe the central part of the second dimension of faith is *commitment*. Consider for a moment the analogy to marriage vows. The willingness of a couple to establish what is surely one of life's most sacred relationships is clearly based on a high level of confidence in each other. This is what I earlier called "creedence," that each is worthy of all the other can give. But the wedding oath goes beyond a declaration of this verdict, which is based largely on evidence from the past, by pledging love and loyalty for a lifetime, most of which is yet to come in the future. Likewise, it is one thing to affirm that the claims of Christ for the past two thousand years are trustworthy, but it is quite another thing to say that *I* will trust Him from this day forward, come what may. Here we see how faith, like repentance, takes the future very seriously. To say that I am committed to Christ implies not only that the goal of my life is the kingdom of God but also that I am counting on Him to get me there regardless of where the road may lead.

Faith as Communion with the Reality of Christ

Once we form a relationship without any reservations, our unconditional commitment unleashes enormous possibilities for growth. If our personality has boundless potential within itself, how much more do two personalities creatively interacting have to offer each other—especially when one of them is the Son of God! When that open-ended growth begins to take place, its fruit is *intimacy,* a word that makes us nervous because of the depths which it sounds. Some would reserve such a term for marriage by making it a synonym for sexual union, but physical intercourse is no guarantee of personal intimacy—else why so many divorces by people who have been living together for years? True intimacy is the high goal of every significant interpersonal relationship.

Experts on human intimacy have long recognized that its achievement is not a matter of how long or how much two people have shared but of how deeply their needs are met by each other. The issue is not one of sentimentality but of intensity. Intimacy springs from risking fresh openness after a relationship becomes routine, from being present to each other with heightened awareness, from caring for each other with deepened trust, from understanding each other with instinctive rapport. The result is not the loss of one's individuality but the gain of a shared identity, what T. S. Eliot made one of his characters exclaim—"The new person—us!"[1] To reclaim a worn-out word, intimacy is marked by a sense of *togetherness* that pervades the whole of one's relationship to another.

Applied to the third dimension of faith, spiritual intimacy means an intense cultivation of the mind and spirit and will of Christ. It is not so much a matter of talking about Him all of the time as it is a conscious yielding to His presence until "I live, yet not I, but Christ lives in me" (see Gal. 2:20). This kind of language is sometimes said to refer to the "mystical union" of Christ and the believer. Mystical union means a communion in which two hearts beat as one, two minds think as one, two wills act as one. Unlike the mysticism of the Eastern religions where the human being is absorbed, Christ mysticism allows us to remain fully ourselves since the integrity of neither partner is ever confused.[2]

The supreme key to true intimacy is love, which is why Paul described the only thing that matters as "faith working through love" (Gal. 5:6; compare Eph. 3:17; 6:23; 1 Thess. 1:3; 3:6; 2 Thess. 1:3; Philem. 5). Love enables faith to soar far beyond submission, beyond even obedience, to become a knitting, a bonding, a coupling of two spirits as closely as two bodies are joined in marriage (1 Cor. 6:17). The two very different natures of Christ and the Christian remain distinct, yet they finally merge at the level of intention so that the Christian *wants* to live as one with Christ. Once motives begin to merge, then Christlike character and conduct soon follow. The Savior literally becomes our alter ego or second self, the living center of our very being.

Having reached this climactic point, we are now ready to grasp the meaning of faith in all of the major stages of its unfolding. Viewed as a whole, we may describe faith as the process by which we form an authentic relationship with Jesus Christ (that is, one that is open, honest, and growing). As such, we have seen that faith includes: (1) a conviction that the claims of Christ are credible, primarily because of the quality of the witness to them from the past; (2) a commitment to share our ongoing life with Christ in loyalty and trust, primarily because of a confidence that He is humanity's most reliable guide to the future; and (3) a communion with Him in love that shapes the very structure of character, primarily because our mystical union with Christ permits Him to live through us in the present.

Since this is the nature of faith, I conclude that it speaks to the deepest need of human nature: Neither the "will to pleasure" (Sigmund Freud) nor the "will to power" (Alfred Adler) nor even the "will to meaning" (Victor Frankl) but the *will to relate*.[3] All of our hungers for affection, for recognition, for significance are satisfied only in relationship and, by making faith central, that is the way in which Scripture says that we may be saved! Every drive to self-actualization finally means nothing if it is achieved in isolation. Thus, just as repentance by its nature saves us from despair, so faith by its nature saves us from loneliness. We may or may not be close to family or friends, but the gospel declares that we can be close to Christ! By means of faith, He is no longer ancient history but immediate presence, no longer static dogma but unfolding truth, no longer timeless example but restless love. With Christ, life is never empty at its center. No wonder the New Testament affirms, *"Believe* in the Lord Jesus, and you will be *saved"* (Acts 16:31, author's italics).

Notes

1. Howard J. Clinebell, Jr., and Charlotte H. Clinebell, *The Intimate Marriage* (New York: Harper and Row, 1970), p. 33, citing T. S. Eliot, *The Cocktail Party* (New York: Harcourt, Brace, 1950), p. 137.

2. Adolf Deissmann, *Paul: A Study in Social and Religious History* (New York: Harper and Brothers Publishers, 1957), pp. 144-157.

3. Clinebell and Clinebell, pp. 12-13.

Bibliography

Clements, Keith W. *Faith*. London: SCM Press, 1981. 126 pages. Ebeling, Gerhard. *The Nature of Faith*. Translated by Ronald Gregor Smith. Philadelphia: Fortress Press, 1967. 192 pages.

Hermisson, Hans-Jürgen and Eduard Lohse. *Faith*. Translated by Douglas W. Stott. Biblical Encounters Series. Nashville: Abingdon Press, 1981. 176 pages.

Oldham, J. H. *Life Is Commitment*. London: SCM Press, 1953. 140 pages.

Oldham. J. H. *Real Life Is Meeting*. Greenwich: Seabury Press, 1953 [first published in Great Britain in 1942]. 80 pages.

4

Confession

To those primarily acquainted with churches that emphasize a public profession of faith, confession is one of the most confusing and controversial aspects of the salvation experience. To begin with, such churches seem to be neglecting confession at just the time when the world is discovering it. After persons "come down the aisle" to make a profession of faith, they are usually asked to fill out a membership card which is then interpreted to the people by the pastor. At the time of baptism, the candidates are again silent as the pastor pronounces the words administering the ordinance. In many congregations, it is possible to join the church without opening one's mouth. Since many churches do not use historic confessions of faith as a part of their services of worship, it is safe to say that a host of members live out their lives without ever "confessing" anything about themselves, whether good or bad, either in private or in public.

Contrast that, if you will, with what Charles Krauthammer has called our "Mea Culpa Generation,"[1] of those who "tell it like it is" and "let it all hang out." There are television talk-show hosts who have become father or mother confessor of a host of "personalities" seeking celebrity status by indulging in confessional overkill on camera before millions of strangers. Prominent politicians have learned to display "character" by accepting full responsibility for everything while neglecting to take the blame or make amends for anything. Think of the Watergate villains. Most of them rushed their every indiscretion into print as soon as they had milked the lecture circuit dry. This confessional chic by those who play the penitence-for-pay game has become commercialized. It threatens to drive any sensitive person into taking a vow of privacy never to engage in religious exhibitionism which would feed the ego of some high-pressure preacher.

Even within Christianity, major denominations differ over the place of confession in the experience of salvation. Some suspect that any insistence on "coming down the aisle" is a subtle form of salvation by works. They see it primarily as a matter of human initiative, that is, as something an individual does to gain God's favor. When that response is urged in the most emotional terms possible by a fervent preacher, especially in the context of mass evangelism, they become even more convinced that salvation is being confused with salesmanship.

Here, then, are at least three problems to be faced in understanding confession as a vital part of the salvation experience: (1) How can we lift it above the rather passive routine of coming-down-the-aisle-and-being-baptized and view it instead as a lifetime calling to bear active witness to the saving work of God in Jesus Christ? (2) How can we honor the desire for privacy on the part of those reacting against the pop penitence of the soap-opera salvation so common in the mass media and still give mature faith enough visibility so that Christianity will be a potent force in contemporary public life? (3) How can we take a stand for Christ, and urge others to do the same, without becoming proud of what we have done or what we have convinced others to do? In short, how can we make confession a God-centered rather than a self-centered experience in our lives?

The answers to these and related questions will obviously come only by grounding our understanding of confession in the significance which it has in the Bible. We have seen that when Jesus proclaimed the gospel of repentance and faith (Mark 1:14-15), He immediately called disciples to follow Him (vv. 16-18). Consider the implications of this strategy: (1) Repentance and faith were not to remain inward and individualistic but were to be given outward expression in a corporate body of believers. (2) The decision to "follow" (that is, to turn life in the direction that Jesus was going because of trust in His leadership for the future), was not prompted by the inward disposition of the disciples but by the sovereign initiative of Christ. (3) Proof that the entire venture was controlled by the Leader rather than by the followers is seen in the fact that He, not they, determined who would belong to the disciple band. Membership was not a matter of human preference but of Christ's electing grace (John 15:16).

How different all of this was to Judaism! In the system those ancient Galileans had inherited, one was born into the people of God and, if a male, so marked for a lifetime by circumcision. The kingdom of God was promised to Israel by the covenant; one did not have to choose it by repentance and faith or affiliation with some rabbi's band. But Jesus transcended every tie of nation and family and land. He said that the kingdom of God was inward (Luke 17:21) and that only those who sought it with all their hearts would find it (Matt. 6:33). This radical inwardness of Jesus' message shattered the solidarity which every Jew had felt for centuries with the Chosen People, yet Jesus dared to replace that relationship with a personal attachment to Himself. Not physical kinship with Abraham but confessing Christ before others became the test of whether one would some day inherit the kingdom of God (Matt. 10:32-33).

Now we begin to see the necessity for confession in the gospel of Jesus Christ. At least three functions are involved. First, confession offers outward *confirmation* of the inward experiences of repentance and faith by relating those spiritual attitudes to a concrete act of the total person. Second, it provides a community for a commitment which at first was only personal by bonding the believer to a community which shares the same convictions. Third, it provokes human *controversy* by declaring in word and in deed the unrecognized but revolutionary salvation of God is already at work in our world. As for those time factors which form the backdrop of every salvation experience, we may say that the confirmation which relates confession to the self deals primarily with the *past;* the community commitment which relates confession to others deals primarily with the *present;* and the controversy which relates confession to God deals primarily with the *future.* Let us now explore in more detail what each of these categories means.

Confession as Confirmation

Everything that I have summarized about the experience of salvation up to this point lies under the threat of limiting it to being only a personal feeling. Think back on earlier chapters: All that was said about each stage in the process of repenting and believing happens deep within the individual heart, so how can we be sure that we are not deceiving ourselves? How can we answer the charge of skeptics that salvation is merely a form of wishful thinking? Very early in church history there emerged groups called Gnostics who wanted to make Christianity entirely inward. Like some of the Oriental religions flooding America today, gnosticism was a form of salvation based on self-understanding. The church has always rejected as heretical any emphasis that would cut Christianity loose from its ties with history and society.

Confession enables our experience of salvation to escape from the limitations of personal impressions. Psychologists have long known that, when our feelings remain repressed deep inside the consciousness, they are subject to tremendous distortion. Once they drop down into the unconscious to mingle with our fantasies and daydreams, they are no longer open to clarification and correction because they are never subjected to scrutiny by others. To confess is to expose our spiritual condition to the clear light of day, to search for words that express our experiences in ways that others can understand, and to get what has happened to us out into the open. We do this so that we ourselves can view it with a measure of objectivity and decide if we are satisfied with what we see. Confession, in this sense, is really a strategy for keeping our religion honest, a plea for insight from those who have no vested interest in our situation and, therefore, can be more realistic in their appraisal of it.

We are called to confess our sins (1 John 1:9) and our faith (Rom. 10:9). In regard to the former, confession is a way of lifting sin out of seclusion. Evil is an active force in human existence. To be shut up with it alone is to be utterly vulnerable. Satan wants to isolate each victim, to lurk undiscovered, to dwell in the darkness of a closed life. As long as we harbor sin in the heart, a heart which the Bible says "is deceitful above all things" (Jer. 17:9), we will indulge in endless camouflage and subterfuge. But when we confess our sins, we expose them to the relentless glare of the gospel. Sin is a darkness (1 John 2:11) that cannot endure gospel light. Evil begins to lose its grip just as soon as it can no longer drive us to deception or puff our pride or poison us with suspicion. The very act of confession is a deliberate declaration of openness to the possibility of forgiveness—which is the one thing that sin cannot survive! Confession is a cry for help from beyond, a frank admission that we need what only God can offer.

What makes this confession of sin more than a guilt trip is the fact that with it we are also called to acknowledge the gracious action of God in responding to our plea (see Ps. 32:3-5). In the New Testament, confession becomes a celebration of how our salvation was completed in Jesus Christ (Phil. 2:11). Christ Himself actually becomes the content of our confession (Heb. 3:1)—that is, we confess not *who* we are but *whose we* are.[2]

What we have learned in this section is that the tongue is a crucial test of what is really going on deep inside of us. As the Letter of James shrewdly observed, the mouth is like a spring pouring forth the kind of water found in the stream that feeds it (3:11-12). If all we ever talk about is the weather and politics and petty gossip, then we must question whether any divine realities are at work within us. For when the miracle of salvation has actually *happened* to us, then the word of it will be "on our lips" (Rom. 10:8).

But confession does more than clarify our inward experiences by turning them into outward explanations. It also confirms who we really are by requiring us to take responsibility for our open witness. As Gabriel Marcel has observed, all testimony is ultimately "under oath" whether or not we swear to it in a court of law.[3] For only I can disclose what I have experienced, hence I am the guarantor of its truthfulness. My very identity is bound up with my self-disclosures. In the last analysis, only I am answerable for my assertions about salvation. Therefore, to say nothing is to sidestep any responsibility, while to bear witness is to speak a "binding word" that cannot be retrieved. In making a public pledge, I accept the obligation of fidelity, an obligation which I can discharge only by embodying that witness in my life. Stated simply: Some people say nothing by way of confession because nothing has happened to them, while others say nothing for fear that they will have to back up their words with their lives. Do you want to be guilty of silence for either of these reasons?

Confession as Community Commitment

In approaching this section, you need to know the root meaning of the verb "to confess" as used in the New Testament. The original Greek term is a compound of a verbal stem meaning "word," and a prefix meaning "same." Therefore, the literal meaning of the term is "to say the same thing as" in the sense of "to agree with." Used religiously, "to confess" means to declare the same testimony as others by affirming a common faith. In other words, the term itself is inherently social. Confession does not mean to make a solitary declaration but rather to join oneself to a community by agreeing with its corporate testimony. If repentance and faith refer to the process by which salvation is genuinely personalized in the inward experience of the individual, then confession refers to the process by which salvation is genuinely socialized in the shared experience of the group.

What this means, of course, is that we are not required to figure out the meaning of our salvation in solitude. As soon as we begin to search for words to express its significance, we find that a host of others have already found a language to describe the same experience, a "confession of faith" which has been refined and enriched over centuries of worship and reflection. Thus we may enter into the solidarity of these shared convictions with the reassurance that our experience has been verified, and thereby reinforced, by countless fellow pilgrims who preceded us on the Way. At the same time, we may bring our distinctive experience to the group in the confidence that we enrich its collective witness by adding one more link to the great chain of living testimony stretching across so many generations. Thus, in confession we both strengthen and are strengthened by the faith of the church in all times and places.

But the ministry of confession extends far beyond that of mutual reinforcement. For this believing community in which we dare to disclose our deepest experiences exists not to criticize or condemn but to support and forgive. Christ realized that divine forgiveness was so deeply spiritual that He delegated to His followers the awesome responsibility of expressing it to others in human relationships. No one can forgive sins like those who pray every day to be forgiven by God as they forgive others (Matt. 6:12, 14-15). How much better it is to confess our sins to fellow Christians (Jas. 5:16) in a context of worship where God is present (1 Cor. 14:24-25) than it is to attempt some sort of autoforgiveness by confessing our sins to ourselves. For now a fellowship of sinners not only forgives our sins in the name of Christ but also joins with us to fight against our sins for as long as we shall live.

To be sure, we must learn to accept ourselves, which is always difficult to do because we are so painfully aware of our shortcomings. No matter how open and honest we try to be, we never confess to others the worst that we know about ourselves. For that reason, we are always harder on ourselves than on anyone else. Jesus knew that we are more willing to forgive others than we are to forgive ourselves. Therefore He did not speak of learning self-acceptance but of learning to forgive others and to be forgiven by them. For He understood that it was in the strength of being accepted by others that we learn to accept ourselves. Confession is crucial because it is the breakthrough to that kind of community in which we can be forgiven so completely, so honestly, so joyfully, that eventually we learn to forgive others and, at last, even to forgive ourselves. Without this group affirmation of our worth prompted by confession, we never break out of the cycle of self-accusation which is our ultimate despair.

Confession as Controversy

Because we confess not ourselves but the Christ who lives within us (compare 2 Cor. 4:5), our witness is a word from the beyond which challenges the secular mind-set. By testifying to the presence of salvation at the center of our lives, we do battle against the counternotion that ours is a world without God. This confession anticipates the future by declaring *now* what is *yet* to be, namely, that "Jesus Christ is Lord" (Rom. 10:9). At present only believers acknowledge His sovereignty, but the day will come when every tongue shall confess His cosmic lordship (Phil. 2:11). By insisting that the future will be completely different from the present, we dare to undermine the permanence of the status quo. Because our confession is God-given, it does not echo the human consensus but comes, when necessary, as an alien voice pointing to realities which the world is not yet ready to accept.

This adversarial nature of our confession is based upon the fact that the devil "has nothing to do with the truth, because there is no truth in him. When he lies, he speaks according to his own nature, for he is a liar and the father of lies" (John 8:44). Because Satan rules in so many lives, our world is full of distortions and downright falsehoods. This means that there is inevitable conflict between the kingdom of evil and those determined to tell the truth, especially about God. Genuine confession is prompted by the Holy Spirit (1 Cor. 12:3), but over against this is false confession prompted by "the spirit of antichrist" (1 John 4:1-3). Some Christians seem to think that their witness should be eagerly accepted by everyone because it concerns such a wonderful Savior, hence they feel rebuffed when that is often not the case. What they fail to realize is that their testimony is a denial of the false values by which many people live and which they will not give up without a fight.

Alexander Solzhenitsyn has spoken powerfully of this controversial dimension of confession out of his vocation as a writer in exile: "What can literature possibly do against the ruthless onslaught of open violence? Let us not forget that violence does not exist by itself and cannot do so; it is necessarily interwoven with lies. Violence finds its only refuge in falsehood, falsehood its only support in violence. . . . But writers and artists . . . can conquer the lie. In the struggle with falsehood, art has always won and always will win! One word of truth shall outweigh the whole world." [4]

The victory of truth over falsehood does not come either quickly or easily, however. Thus our confession cannot be based on the optimism that it will be readily accepted. Instead, confession is a lifelong obligation which we must discharge because the reality to which we point is not our own but is a gift from God that is true whether anyone else recognizes and accepts it as such. Elie Wiesel tells about a righteous man who went to the sinful city of Sodom, determined to save its inhabitants from destruction.

> Night and day he walked the streets and markets preaching against greed and theft, falsehood and indifference. In the beginning people listened and smiled ironically. Then they stopped listening; he no longer even aroused them. The killers went on killing, the wise kept silent, as if there were no just man in their midst.
>
> One day a child, moved by compassion for the unfortunate preacher, approached him with these words: "Poor stranger, you shout, you expend yourself body and soul; don't you see that is hopeless?"
>
> "Yes, I see," answered the Just Man.
>
> "Then why do you go on?"
>
> "I'll tell you why. In the beginning, I thought that I could change man. Today, I know I cannot. If I still shout today, if I still scream, it is to prevent man from ultimately changing me!"[5]

In this chapter we have been concerned with the place of confession in the experience of salvation. The relationship between the two is best defined by Romans 10:9-10. Paul began by identifying confession as a condition of salvation ("If you confess with your lips . . . you will be saved," v. 9), but ended by describing confession as an expression of salvation (v. 10). The original Greek literally says, "With the lips confession is made *unto salvation*." That is, by means of confession one reaches out for a salvation that is essentially future and makes it a part of present experience by putting it into words. The point in not that "saying something makes it so"; rather, the point is that salvation is already so and *may be experienced insofar as it is confessed!*

The greatest realities in life are invisible: love, courage, patriotism. But love has its kiss, courage has its medals of valor, patriotism has its flag to embody the unseen realities which they express. The most invisible reality of all is God, but even He became visible in the life of Jesus Christ. The "word made flesh" (see John 1:14) was God's confession to humanity of His deepest nature. Just so, when we confess our faith to others, the invisible salvation within our hearts becomes a public word which permits others to hear and believe. Such confession does not so much describe God or explain God or commend God as it conveys God, confronts us with His claims, and meditates His living presence.

No wonder Sören Kierkegaard wrote in his journal:

> There is something quite definite I have to say, and I have it so much upon my conscience that (as I feel) I dare not die without having uttered it. For the instant I die and thus leave this world (so I understand it) I shall in the same second be infinitely far away, in a different place where still within the same second the question will be put to me: "Hast thou uttered the definite message *quite definitely?*" And if I have not done so, what then?[6]

Notes

1. Charles Krauthammer, "The Mea Culpa Generation," *The New Republic*, February 21, 1981, pp. 17-19.

2. Elton Trueblood, *The Company of the Committed* (New York: Harper & Brothers, 1961), p. 54.

3. Gabriel Marcel, *The Philosophy of Existence* (London: Harvell Press, 1948), pp. 67-70.

4. Cited in *Time*, September 4, 1972, p. 33.

5. Cited by Martin E. Marty, *Context*, January 15, 1976, p. 6, from a sermon by Rabbi Simeon Maslin.

6. Cited by James S. Stewart, *A Faith to Proclaim* (London: Hodder and Stoughton, 1953), p. 36.

Bibliography

Bowman, III, George William. *The Dynamics of Confession*. Richmond: John Knox Press, 1969. 125 pages.

Marcel, Gabriel. "Testimony," *The Mystery of Being, II: Truth and Reality*. Chicago: Henry Regnery Company, 1951. Pages 125-145.

Marcel, Gabriel. "Testimony and Existentialism," *The Philosophy of Existence*. London: Harvell Press, 1948. Pages 67-76.

Stott, John R. W. *Confess Your Sins: The Way of Reconciliation*. Philadelphia: Westminster Press, 1965. 92 pages.

Thurneysen, Eduard. "Evangelical Confession," *Preaching, Confession, The Lord's Supper*. Richmond: John Knox Press, 1960. Pages 39-77.

Trueblood, Elton. "The Vocation of Witness," *The Company of the Committed*. New York: Harper & Brothers, 1961. Pages 45-67.

Part II
The Change

How often do we hear the old saying, "Human nature never changes." Just the other day a friend explained that his viewpoint was very different from mine because "I'm not wired up the way you are," as if we were each obedient to some internal mechanism which could not be altered. Many years ago an elderly deacon in our church became deeply offended with his daughter-in-law whom he felt had wronged him without cause. When I, as pastor, urged him to take a loving initiative to restore their broken relationship, he exploded, "To do that is just not human nature!" "True," I replied, "but now you have a Christian nature!"

At precisely this point we confront one of the deepest paradoxes in our experience of salvation. The apostle Paul put it simply: "I live; yet not I" (Gal. 2:20, KJV). On the one hand, Paul did *not* live because he had been "crucified with Christ." On the other hand he *did* live because the resurrected Christ lived "in him." What this "I-yet-not-I" paradox affirms as strongly as possible is that *human nature can be changed!* This transformation of one's innermost being has two aspects: (1) the old nature is destroyed just as surely as Christ was killed on the cross, and (2) a new nature is given life just as surely as Christ was raised from the dead. Nor could the two natures be more different: The former is self-centered while the latter is Christ-centered.

But merely to affirm the *fact* of change does not determine the *extent* to which such change is possible in our earthly lives. We have already seen in Part I that by repentance we gain a new direction, by faith we gain a new relationship, and by confession we gain a new community. But even after making all of these choices we are still left with the same body, the same habits, the same heritage, the same circumstances. Clearly some things are changed by salvation and some are not. Unless we can distinguish rather clearly between the two, we will always be in danger

53

either of claiming too much or of claiming too little for the salvation which we experience in Christ.

The purpose of Part II is to examine the changes that actually do, and do not, occur when one repents, believes, and confesses Christ. Balancing the three chapters of Part I will be treatments of the three basic clusters of word pictures used in the New Testament to describe how salvation alters human existence. First, chapter 5 will consider what it means for each Christian to be viewed as a new creation. This will be done by surveying the terminology used to describe how our very being is transformed through the saving work of Christ. Next, in chapter 6 I shall set the individual in a larger context by showing how believers are adopted into the family of God, a status which makes them heirs of an inheritance yet to be received. Finally, in chapter 7, I shall focus on the comprehensive biblical concept of conversion in order to explore both the possibilities and the limits of living out our newness in a largely unchanged world.

As the three chapters of Part II unfold, it is important to hold them in balance with the three chapters of Part I. At first glance, Part I seems to concentrate on human choices, as if salvation were primarily a matter of what we do, while Part II seems to concentrate on divine changes, as if salvation were primarily a matter of what God does. A closer look will show that all of our choices are prompted by God and that all of His changes are permitted by us. *Choice and change are inseparable aspects of the salvation experience!* The decisions of a lifetime mean little unless they permit God to work with supernatural impact in our lives. Conversely, the miraculous power of the gospel means little unless it moves us to open our lives to its claims.

Some theologians have tried to exalt God by insisting that He is sovereign in the sense of being able to save us entirely apart from our participation in the process. Some humanists have reacted to that view by insisting, at the other extreme, that we should take full responsibility for our destiny entirely apart from God's participation in the process. By combining the doctrines discussed in Part I with those now to be considered in Part II, you should be able to avoid either of these distortions. As you read the next three chapters, marvel at what God, and God alone, can do if only we, and we alone, will let Him have full sway in our lives.

5
Regeneration

Out of his vast study of humanity's spiritual quest through many centuries and in many cultures, Mircea Eliade has written:

> . . . at a certain moment every man sees his life as a failure. This vision does not arise from a moral judgment made on his past, but from an obscure feeling that he has . . . betrayed the best that was in him. In such moments of total crisis, only one hope seems to offer any issue—the hope of beginning life over again.[1]

Every one of us comes to experience that sense of listlessness, of weariness, of decay at the heart of human existence. Life itself often seems to be one long process of dying. Sight dims, hearing fades, organs fail, and the aging of the body signals its inevitable demise. But relationships also wither, opportunities shrivel, the zest for adventure wanes, and we seem caught in a kind of spiritual entropy—to borrow a word used by scientists to refer to the degradation of matter when its energy is dissipated.

And when that happens, when vitality seems to ebb from the soul, we must counter it with an upsurge of fresh energy or the spiritual life will finally collapse. Joseph Campbell has written: "Only birth can conquer death. . . . Within the soul, within the body social, there must be . . . a continuous 'recurrence of birth' to nullify the unremitting recurrences of death."[2] But where shall we find that perpetual source of renewal that permits us to "begin life over again"? According to the Bible, it is to be found most deeply in the Christian experience of regeneration.

The Symbols of Regeneration

In seeking to point to the reality of regeneration in human life, the Scriptures parade a series of pictures before our eyes, visible analogies of the unseen transformation which can take place deep within. All of them depict the way in which new life rushes in to fill the void created by "the unremitting recurrences of death." They share in common the fundamental faith that God "gives life to the dead and calls into existence the things that do not exist" (Rom. 4:17). Two of the three most important images of how this process works are drawn from nature, suggesting that God has built into creation a kind of sign language which declares His intention to make of our lives a new creation.

The Symbol of Procreation

The most basic metaphor for regeneration is that of birth. As Carl Sandburg put it, "A baby is God's opinion that life should go on."[3] In the case of Abraham and Sarah, his body "was as good as dead" and her womb had long been barren because of their advanced age. But God had promised that Abraham would be "the father of many nations," and He kept that promise by giving the couple an offspring as a sign of His miraculous power (Rom. 4:18-21). In situations just as hopeless today, when our hearts are as barren as the womb of Sarah, spiritual birth can take place "not of blood nor of the will of the flesh nor of the will of man [that is, not of human effort], but of God" (John 1:13).

Jesus made this new birth by divine begetting a crucial theme in His message of salvation. In the Gospel of John, Jesus demanded of Nicodemus, and of the Jewish leaders whom he represented, that they be born a second time from above (John 3:1-7). To people proud of the way in which they had been physically born into the commonwealth of Israel (Phil. 3:4-5; Eph. 2:11-12), Jesus insisted that they must also be spiritually reborn if they wished to so much as glimpse the kingdom of God. In the Synoptic Gospels, He urged young and old alike to "become as little children" (see Matt. 18:3; Mark 10:15; Luke 18:17), which obviously could not happen unless they began life all over again. Based on the conviction of Jesus that reproduction is just as real in the spiritual realm as in the physical realm (John 3:6), 1 Peter 1:3 describes salvation as having "been *born anew* to a living hope"(author's italics).

The Symbol of Germination

Our second image shifts from the obstetrical to the agricultural or, as we would put it today, from the hospital to the farm. That connection was quite natural to the biblical writers. In the Old Testament, one's progeny was regularly referred to as one's "seed"; for example, the "seed of

Abraham" meant Abraham's offsprings and descendants. In the New Testament, the Greek word *sperma* could mean either "semen" or "seed." Jesus used many parables to describe the potency of seed to multiply all out of proportion to its size. The divine arithmetic is "thirty-fold and sixtyfold and a hundredfold" (Mark 4:8). Just so, our souls are like soil which, when planted and cultivated, may yield a bountiful harvest not of our making (Mark 4:3-8,26-32). In 1 Peter 1:23 the generative and germinative images are united in the declaration, "You have been *born anew,* not of perishable seed but *of imperishable* [*seed*]"(author's italics).

The Symbol of Resurrection

In one sense, the rebirth of nature each spring is like a resurrection from the dead. As the green grass begins to push up through barren soil, as buds begin to appear on empty limbs, we should be moved to pray, "God, do something like that inside of me." But there is an example of resurrection that goes beyond anything in the natural order—the return of Jesus Christ from the dead. When we identify with that event by faith, literally acting out our own death, burial, and resurrection in the waters of baptism, then Christ is raised to new life *in us* (Rom. 6:4-5; Eph. 2:1,5; Col. 2:12). The only thing more lifeless than the aged Sarah's womb was the crucified Jesus' tomb. Nor can we deny that our hearts sometimes seem like a graveyard of buried hopes. But just as God rolled away the stone from Jesus' tomb that new life might come forth, so He enables us to be "born anew . . . through the *resurrection* of Jesus Christ from the dead (1 Pet. 1:3, author's italics).

In one sense these three images are quite different: a baby emerging from the womb, a seed emerging from the soil, a corpse emerging from the grave. But they all have one crucial thing in common: *the appearance of new life where it did not exist before!* The apostle Paul gathered up all of these metaphors for transformation into the comprehensive concept of new creation (2 Cor. 5:17; Gal. 6:15). By this doctrine he affirmed that every person connected to Christ is so totally changed that the resulting life is wholly original: "The old has passed away, behold, the new has come" (2 Cor. 5:17). Further, by calling the Christian a "new creation" rather than simply a new person or even a new humanity, Paul implied that the changes already at work in the believer's life are integral parts of a process by which God will finally renovate the entire universe in accordance with His will and purpose.

The Sources of Regeneration

All three of the symbols just surveyed stress human helplessness to originate new life. It was laughable to think that either Abraham or Sarah could do anything to overcome her barrenness (Gen. 17:17; 18:11-12). Once the farmer had planted and cultivated, he could only wait for the seed to multiply in and of itself (Mark 4:27). The followers of Jesus gave up in despair once His lifeless body had been sealed in the tomb (John 16:32; 21:3). But even though God alone can call into being that which is not, He does use processes that accommodate His power to the human scene, thereby allowing believers to cooperate with Him as agents of new life. Let us look now at three factors stressed in Scripture as sources of divine transformation in human life.

The Word

Jesus likened the preaching of the gospel to the scattering of seed (Mark 4:14). Once the "word of truth" is implanted in our lives, we become "a kind of first fruits" of God's harvest rather than a "rank growth" of weeds and thorns (Jas. 1:18,21). Because the "word of the Lord abides for ever" (see Isa. 40:8), 1 Peter can claim that we are "born anew, not of perishable seed but of imperishable, through the *living and abiding word* of God" (1:23, author's italics). Because preachers of the gospel participate in the broadcasting of the word-as-seed, they function somewhat as earthly parents in relation to those who are spiritually reborn as a result of their efforts (1 Cor. 4:15; Gal. 4:19).

The Wind

One of the most impressive visions of regeneration in the Old Testament is found in Ezekiel 37. There the prophet was shown a valley full of dead bones, symbolizing the lifeless house of Israel in Exile. The central question posed by such a sight was, obviously, "Can these bones live?" (v. 3). God's answer to the need for renewal was twofold. First, Ezekiel was to say to those dry bones, "Hear the word of the Lord" (v. 4). But then God added that He would cause "breath" to enter the bones and animate them (v. 5). This promise was fulfilled as Ezekiel prophesied on behalf of God, "Come from the four winds, O breath, and breathe upon these slain, that they may live" (v. 9). Throughout the passage there is a constant play on words because the Hebrew term *ruah* can mean "spirit," "breath," or "wind."

Jesus alluded to this experience of Ezekiel in an effort to explain the new birth to Nicodemus (John 3:1-8). When this cautious leader questioned how persons could change so drastically once they were old and set in their ways (see v. 4), Jesus replied that anything is possible when one is "born of the Spirit" (vv. 5-7). He then illustrated His teaching by reminding Nicodemus of the unfettered freedom of the wind to "blow where it wills" (see v. 8). Once again the same play on words is at work because the Greek term *pneuma*, like its Hebrew equivalent, can also mean "spirit," "breath," or "wind." What both passages suggest is that God's Spirit is a prime source of new life (Rom. 8:2). Just as a person being rescued from drowning has breath forced down into oxygen-starved lungs through mouth-to-mouth resuscitation, so God breathes directly into our spiritually starved lives and we are saved "by the washing of regeneration and *renewal in the Holy Spirit*" (Titus 3:5, author's italics).

The Water

As the reference to "the washing of regeneration" just quoted indicates, water is a symbol of the deep-seated change needed in our lives. When something is new it is unusually clean, pure, and undefiled. Just so, the Christian confession takes place in the waters of baptism, a symbol of spiritual cleansing. When Nicodemus resisted the teaching of Jesus on becoming a new creation, he was reminded that one must be "born *of water* and the Spirit" in order to enter the kingdom of God (John 3:5, author's italics). In the original historical context, this mention of water may have been a reference to the baptism of John, who had already called his fellow Jews to begin all over again in the waters of the Jordan River (John 1:19,24). Later, the apostle Paul pointed to baptism as a symbol of the Holy Spirit's washing that cleansed his converts of the grossest immoralities (1 Cor. 6:9-11). Remembering how those in Noah's ark "were saved through water" during the great flood, the apostle Peter went on to state that "baptism, which corresponds to this, now saves you, not as a removal of dirt from the body but as an appeal to God for a clear conscience, through the resurrection of Jesus Christ" (1 Pet. 3:21).

These passages do not teach that the physical water in which we are baptized has any magical power to save. Rather, as we saw in chapter 4, baptism in water is the normative way in which we confess Christ to others and commit ourselves to the community of faith. Therefore, what we learn from considering all three of these sources is that if a person will receive God's word in the preaching of the gospel, will fill heart and life with the Holy Spirit as the lungs are filled with air, and will declare this identification of life with Christ by means of baptism, then that person will make a fresh start in life on a totally new and different basis.

The Significance of Regeneration

Surely the evidence summarized thus far is sufficient to suggest that the *New* Testament is well named, for newness pervades its every page. We constantly encounter hints of that newness in our daily existence. Notice how figures of speech in our language bear witness to the biblical images of change. If the girl of our dreams will just say the right *word* ("I do"), life will never be the same again. If we can just get our second *wind*, maybe we can turn the game around before it ends. If we can just wash some filthy spot with pure *water*, it will come clean at once. What the New Testament adds to these ordinary illustrations of change is the sense that God is ready to work the same kind of experiences in our spiritual lives if only we will let Him. If transformation is taking place in the natural order every time a baby is born, every time a seed is planted, every time winter gives way to spring, then why shouldn't an even greater change be possible every time we allow the Holy Spirit to fill our lives? Or, to ask it another way, since God completely reversed the fortunes of the crucified Christ by raising Him from the dead, and since that risen Christ lives in our lives today, then why shouldn't we be able to participate in His stunning triumph?

Clearly the time has come to attempt some explanation for the radical nature of Christian regeneration. And, make no mistake, it *is* radical—a word which means that it gets to the root (Latin *radix* means "root") of the human predicament. There are at least three implications to the doctrine of a God who cries, "Behold, I make all things *new*" (Rev. 21:5, author's italics).

Radical Change

The Christian experience of regeneration declares first that we will never discover the best in life without a radical change at the core of our being. The realm of the spirit and the realm of the flesh are not interchangable; hence if we are to live in them both, we must have not one birth but two (John 3:6). Unlike other religions, Christianity emphasizes not tradition but transformation, not evolution but revolution, not turning over a new leaf but finding a new life. The human pilgrimage is not just incremental, each stage building on the one before; it is also innovative, a new stage departing from what has gone before. Each new moment is actually *new*, offering possibilities that may never have been present to us before.

Radical Growth

By asking us to start life all over again, Christian regeneration carries us back to beginnings, to a point when the adult is but a "little child" and the plant is but a seed. At first this retrogression seems disconcerting—after all, who wants to abandon the hard-won gains of maturity and revert to infancy again? But beginners possess one unique advantage: They have only the future before them without any dead weight from the past to inhibit the opportunities which the future offers. In other words, by returning us to the point of origin, regeneration confronts us with the maximum challenge of growth. We are never allowed even for a moment to suppose that we have arrived or that the end of our striving is at hand (see Phil. 3:12-14). Instead, "like newborn babes [we are to] long for the pure spiritual milk, that by it [we] may grow up to salvation" (1 Pet. 2:2).

Radical Hope

Finally, once we dare to start life all over again, we are given not only a new future in which to grow but also "a living hope" (1 Pet. 1:3) as to where that growth will lead. When we look back to the past, we remember "the futile ways inherited from [our] fathers" (v. 18), but now we have been delivered from this fateful legacy "to an inheritance which is imperishable, undefiled, and unfading" (v. 4). If, like Nicodemus, we cling only to the first birth of flesh, then our hope is limited to human achievement. But if by a second birth of the Spirit we are open to all that Christ will yet accomplish, then our "faith and hope are in God" (v. 21). A Christian lives with confidence that the best is yet to be!

All of us like to get something new: a new home, a new car, a new outfit. Therefore, it seems that we would jump at the chance to get a new life. W. H. Auden cautioned us against easy optimism by having one of his characters say:

> We would rather be ruined than changed,
> We would rather die in our dread
> Than climb the cross of the moment
> And let our illusions die.[4]

We pay a high price for change drastic enough to deliver us from death. Nothing less is required than to shift life from human control to divine control. It is not easy to forsake familiar patterns and live in openness to constant surprise. The passage from life in the flesh to life in the Spirit is as traumatic as the passage from the womb to this world or from the tomb to the next world. The essence of change is unpredictability, but that is a risk we must take. For only when "all things are new" can we live at last in the land of beginning again.

Notes

1. Mircea Eliade, *Birth and Rebirth: The Religious Meanings of Initiation in Human Culture* (New York: Harper & Brothers, 1958), p. 135.

2. Joseph Campbell, *The Hero with a Thousand Faces,* Bollingen Series, XVII (New York: Pantheon Books, 1949), p. 16 cited by John W. Gardner, *Self-Renewal: The Individual and the Innovative Society* (New York: Harper & Row, 1963), p. 123.

3. Carl Sandburg, "Remembrance Rock."

4. W. H. Auden, "The Age of Anxiety," *Collected Poems,* edited by Edward Mendelson (New York: Random House, 1976), p. 407.

Bibliography

Burkhardt, Helmut. *The Biblical Doctrine of Regeneration.* Translated by O. R. Johnston. Outreach and Identity: Evangelical Theological Monographs, No. 2. Downers Grove, Ill.: Inter-Varsity Press, 1978. 47 pages.

Godwin, Johnnie C. *What It Means to Be Born Again.* Nashville: Broadman Press, 1977. 138 pages.

6
Adoption

One of the most desperate searches underway in our world today is for babies to adopt. The root of the problem is scarcity caused by an imbalance of supply and demand. On the one hand, involuntary infertility among young couples has increased from 4 percent in 1965 to 11 percent in 1982 while, on the other hand, abortions have removed as many as 1.5 million babies from the potential market each year—which is about equal to the number of infertile couples wishing to adopt. In recent years, there has been a decline of 50 percent in the number of children whom established agencies are able to offer for adoption. Some experts estimate that, in the United States, for every available baby there are at least one hundred couples wanting to adopt. Even for couples who fully qualify after an extensive "home study," the average wait is five to seven years.

In response to this situation, childless couples flock to Charleston, South Carolina, each year in hopes that its less stringent laws and more lenient family court judges will help them to cut through the bureaucratic red tape that hinders the adoption process elsewhere. So insatiable is the demand for newborn babies that a new breed of ambulance chasers has been spawned, the "bassinet hounds" who pursue unwed mothers all the way to the delivery room! Some frustrated couples turn to overseas orphanages, such as those in Colombia, where as many as sixteen thousand homeless children live on the streets of Bogota alone. An elaborate international "adoption underground" has sprung up with its own network of counselors, attorneys, newsletters, and classified ads.[1]

There is an important truth to be learned from this driving desire to adopt a child whom the prospective parents have never seen, whose origins remain shrouded in secrecy, who will require constant attention at enormous cost, who may carry a congenital abnormality or grow up to be a failure. Clearly the drive to adopt reflects one of the deepest hungers of the human heart—*the longing for family,* of adults to have children and of children to belong to parents. Thus we are in touch with a profound current of meaning when we consider how Christianity speaks of our salvation in terms of adoption by God.

The Setting of Adoption

The best place to begin is to set the biblical teachings on divine adoption against an almost empty backdrop. The concept of salvation as incorporation into a heavenly family by adoption is not found in the Old Testament, in intertestamental Judaism, or in the first-century religions of Greece and Rome. The fact that Christianity alone depicted salvation as analogous to adoption suggests that it was unique among the religions of antiquity in its emphasis on the intimately personal relationship of each believer to God.

The main reason adoption was not developed as a religious idea in the Old Testament is the emphasis there on the spiritual significance of natural parentage. Judaism stressed biological continuity from "the seed of Abraham," as may be illustrated by the lengthy genealogies found in 1 and 2 Chronicles. In Romans 9:4, the apostle Paul declared that to his kinsmen, the Israelites, "belong adoption" (the RSV has "sonship"), but he quickly explained in the next verse that this was because "to them belong the patriarchs" (v. 5). In other words, their adoption was based on racial ancestry and so was a matter of "flesh" rather than of choice.

Jesus introduced this distinction into His conversation with Nicodemus by insisting that one who felt spiritually secure because of his natural birth would also need to have a supernatural birth that transcended biological relationships (John 3:3). Implicit in the contrast between being a child of Jewish parents and a child of God (compare John 1:12-13) is a "two family" theology according to which one may transcend the family of flesh by belonging to the family of faith. This, in fact, is what Jesus Himself did in spurning the claims of His earthly family and "adopting," as it were, a spiritual family composed of those who "do the will of God" (Mark 3:31-35, KJV).

The selection of this second family is a matter of personal choice, but that does not mean that we are free to reject a spiritual family and limit ourselves to a physical family. Clearly Jesus taught all of His followers to make God their second or "heavenly" Father (see Matt. 6:9), but Jesus also had enemies who stubbornly refused to allow Him, as the Father's unique Son, to reveal God to them (Matt. 11:27). Of this latter group, He was finally forced to say, "You are of your father the devil and your will is to do your father's desires" (John 8:44). The issue, in other words, is not *whether* we will be adopted but is rather *by whom* we will be adopted, God or Satan?

To summarize: All of us have natural parents over whom we have no choice. These biological progenitors may become the basis for our earthly family, and God may use them for His divine purposes just as He used Abraham in the long ago. But all of us have supernatural parentage as well, and we may choose by faith whether this is to be God or Satan. In either case, that choice of faith causes us, as it were, to be "adopted" into a spiritual family presided over by one or the other of these supernatural "fathers." If our decision is to do the will of God, then we gain many new "relatives" who support us in that commitment (Mark 3:35). But if our decision is to do the works of the devil, then we are reinforced in that allegiance by his many children. In either case, we are "up for adoption" and the choice of parentage will lead either to salvation or to damnation.

The Sequence of Adoption

We usually think of human adoption as an instantaneous change of legal status which comes whenever the proper papers are signed. One moment a couple is childless. The next moment they have a baby all their own! But in actuality, the adoption process may take many months or even years to complete. In like manner, divine adoption is a lifetime process just as is the salvation of which it is an integral part. In fact, in the Bible it is seen to have three distinct stages that stretch from eternity to eternity. We will now examine each of these stages which correspond to the past, present, and future tenses of our Christian experience of salvation.

Divine Adoption in the Past

In Ephesians 1:4-5 we are told that, even "before the foundation of the world" God "destined us in love" for adoption as His children. The Revised Standard Version here has "to be his sons," but the Greek text says literally that God "designated us in advance for adoption." By describing divine "family planning" as having taken place at the beginning of time, Paul was saying that God wanted children for His own, as do childless couples today, before He saw what they would be like! God chose to have a human family, not because certain persons proved to be sweet, adorable, innocent, and pure, but because *from all eternity He has had a father's heart!* The concept of predestination in this passage means that, long before the world was made, God was already working on a plan to make us a part of His family.

The implementation of that plan became visible to us on earth in God's sending of Jesus Christ as His agent of adoption. The whole purpose of Jesus' ministry according to Ephesians 1:5 was that God might adopt children "[*unto Himself*] according to the purpose of his will." The emphatic phrase, which is not highlighted in the Revised Standard Version translation, underscores the determination of God, through the saving work of Christ, to make Christians "his and no one else's children."[2] By the time we learn that we are "up for adoption," we learn at the same time that Christ has loved us to the death as a demonstration of just how much God wants us in His heavenly family.

Divine Adoption in the Present

Once Christ came and completed His work, adoption became a present possibility for every person. The opportunity for adoption was an accomplished fact which "we might *receive*" (Gal. 4:5, author's italics). Paul immediately explained that we could "receive adoption" because "God has sent the Spirit of His Son into our hearts, crying, 'Abba! Father!'" (v. 6). During Jesus' earthly ministry, the spirit that characterized His life was preeminently that of a Son (see for example, Matt. 11:25-27). Now that Jesus is risen, *His* spirit may become *our* spirit so that we dare to use that intimate name for Father, "Abba," which at first only Jesus was close enough to God to use (see for example, Mark 14:36).

With the risen Spirit of Christ, God's son, living in our hearts (Rom. 1:4), we now possess the "spirit of adoption" (Rom. 8:15, KJV; RSV has "spirit of sonship"). This is the antithesis of "the spirit of slavery" which causes one "to fall back into fear" (v. 15). Confidence and security come from knowing "that we are children of God" (v. 16) because "if children, then heirs, heirs of God and fellow heirs with Christ" (v. 17). What the Bible is saying here is that, in salvation, God provides us with all that a family provides a child. Imagine for a moment the plight of a child without any parents, then contrast with that the privileges of a child who has the best parents in the world, and you will begin to understand the change in outlook provided by salvation in Christ.

Divine Adoption in the Future

One of the privileges which parents eventually bestow upon their children is the family inheritance. Through adoption we become "fellow heirs with Christ" of all the blessings that God intends to shower upon His children (Rom. 8:17). But much of this legacy is yet to come in the future. In that sense "we wait for adoption" by hope until the day when our salvation is complete (v. 23). The difference is one of public disclosure. Already we know inwardly that we have been adopted as children of God, but this relationship has not yet been revealed to others (v. 19). Outwardly we seem to be heirs of "the sufferings of this present time" (v. 18). Our bodies die like those of others (Rom. 7:24) because they have not yet been redeemed (Rom. 8:23). We live like commoners in the sight of others when in reality each one of us could shout, "I'm a child of the King."

Now we carry our adoption inwardly, but the day will come when our adoption will be shared with the universe. Now we suffer because Christ still suffers, but one day we shall be glorified as Christ will be glorified (v. 17). Now we groan with the whole creation as it groans (vv. 22-23), but one day the creation will be "set free from its bondage to decay and obtain the glorious liberty" that already belongs to us as children of God (v. 21). Now this eventual transformation is only a hope for the future, and yet it is a hope that has already begun to save us in the present (v. 24). And the key to it all is our adoption by God!

The Significance of Adoption

Most of us have known only natural parents and so have no personal feeling for the urgency of adoption. But imagine for a moment what it would be like to be abandoned on some doorstep as a foundling. In the country of Colombia, a thorough search for parents and relatives lasting three months or more must be completed before an unclaimed infant can be classified as *abandonado* in the eyes of the law. That is where we must begin in order to understand the doctrine of divine adoption. God comes to the rescue because we are spiritually abandoned! deserted! helpless! Without God as our Heavenly Father, we are as spiritually vulnerable as an infant would be without earthly parents or family.

Against that backdrop, we see more clearly that our divine adoption is an act of God's grace. Not every natural child is truly wanted, but we may be certain that every adopted child is urgently desired. Some natural children are said to be "accidents" or "afterthoughts," but adopted children usually are carefully planned, often for several years. Just so, we do not become Christians either by nature or by necessity. Rather, we become Christians because God has planned for us, loved us, and chosen us to be His own.

The result of such lavish grace is a total transformation of our status. In the New Testament world, a well-to-do but childless Greek would often adopt a strong, intelligent slave to perpetuate his name, to care for him in old age, and eventually to receive his inheritance. Thus, literally, would the slave become a son and the son an heir (Gal. 4:7). Paul saw that just such changes take place in the lives of those who are adopted by God to bear His name in the world, to look after His interests throughout the earth, and, at last, to receive the inheritance which He intends for His own.

Because God adopts all who live by the Spirit of His Son, Jesus Christ, our adoption means that we gain not only a new Heavenly Father but also many brothers and sisters. In the last chapter we saw how the transforming power of the gospel works from within in each individual life. But in this chapter we have seen how the changes wrought by salvation give us a new family, new relationships, and, therefore, new social responsibilities. Within the fellowship of faith, we learn to love and care for one another. Homes have often been havens of refuge from the pressures of life, and, by adoption, we have such a place of protection and support as the context in which to nourish our deepest commitments. We may become a *new creation* only one at a time through attachment to Christ (2 Cor. 5:17) but that very connection enables us to become part of a *new community* as dear to us as our closest kin on earth.

Fred Craddock has related how he went back to the place of his roots in East Tennessee for a vacation in Gatlinburg. One evening he and his wife were dining in a restaurant overlooking the Great Smoky Mountains when they saw a distinguished, older gentleman move from table to table greeting guests as if he were the proprietor. Being a stranger on vacation, Craddock somewhat resented the intrusion when the old man finally reached his table and began to talk. Upon learning that Craddock taught preachers at a seminary in Oklahoma, the uninvited visitor replied, "I've got a preacher story to tell you," and with that he pulled up a chair and began to talk.

"I was born just a few miles from here, across the mountain," began his story. "My mother was not married at the time, and the reproach that fell on her soon fell on me as well. They had a name for me when I started to school that was not nice, causing me to stay to myself at recess and lunch times because the taunts cut so deeply. Even worse was to go to town with my mother on Saturday afternoon and feel all of those eyes piercing through me with the question 'Whose child are you?'"

He continued, "When I was about twelve a new preacher came to the little church in our community and I began to attend because of his power and eloquence. I always slipped in late and left early because I was afraid of the look that said, 'What is a boy like you doing in a place like this?' But one Sunday the benediction was over before I realized it, and I found myself caught in a crowd of people heading for the door. Before I could escape I felt a hand on my shoulder and turned to see the preacher looking at me with those burning eyes. 'Who are you, son? Whose boy are you?,' he asked, and I thought to myself, 'Oh, no, here we go again!' But then, as a smile of recognition broke across his face he said, 'Wait a minute. I know who you are. I see the family resemblance. You are a son of God!' And with that he patted me on the rump and said, 'Boy, you've got quite an inheritance. Go and claim it.' That one statement," the old man concluded, "literally changed my whole life."

By now Craddock, utterly enthralled with the story, asked, "Who are you?," and the visitor replied, "Ben Hooper." Then Craddock began to remember that his grandfather used to tell him how, on two different occasions, the people of Tennessee elected one to be their governor who had been born an illegitimate child and his name was Ben Hooper. And he realized, as must we, that even that misfortune could be redeemed by discovering what it means to be a child of God and going out to claim that great inheritance![3]

Notes

1. This summary is based on David Kline, "He's Ours . . . He's Really Ours!" *McCall's,* March, 1984, pp. 57-61, 67; *Time,* March 12, 1984, p. 31; *U. S. News & World Report,* June 25, 1984, p. 62; Kelsey Menehan, "Where Have All the Babies Gone?" *Christianity Today,* October 18, 1985, pp. 26-29.

2. Markus Barth, *Ephesians*, "The Anchor Bible," 34 (Garden City, NY: Doubleday & Company, 1974), vol. 1, p. 80.

3. Related by John R. Claypool, "Children of God: Being or Becoming?," Northminster Baptist Church, Jackson, Mississippi; May 20, 1979, printed sermon, pp. 6-7.

Bibliography

Minear, Paul S. *Jesus and His People*. "World Christian Books." New York: Association
Press, 1956. Pages 44-53.
_____. *Images of the Church in the New Testament*. Philadelphia: Westminster
Press, 1960. Pages 165-172.

7
Conversion

In this second part of our study, we have been looking at various ways in which the Christian experience of salvation brings change to human life. We may now conclude this section by considering the most comprehensive concept used in the Bible to describe saving change, which is *conversion*. The scope of this doctrine covers the entire initial phase of the divine transformation of our existence. Its cruciality can hardly be overestimated: Unless conversion takes place at the "front end" of salvation, not much else may be expected to follow at the "far end" of the process!

The basic meaning of the term *conversion* is that of "turning," from which comes the central idea of "change." This is change in the sense of a "changeover" from one kind of life to another—such as when we speak of "converting" a heating system from coal to natural gas. In general usage, the term means an alteration, substitution, replacement, or exchange. In religious usage, this involves a change of nature by regeneration and a change of identity by adoption. "As James Denney said, it is of the very essence of Christianity that it has in it the power to make bad men good."[1]

And yet, this central claim to be able to change life for the better needs a great deal of clarification. For everything seems constantly to be changing whether we are converted or not. The ancient philosopher Heraclitus once observed that nothing endures but change. In the Victorian era, it was unfashionable to view Christianity as a contributor to that ceaseless flux that leaves life so unstable, hence many people preferred to view God, not as an agent of change, but as a source of constancy:

> Change and decay in all around I see:
> O thou who changest not, abide with me.[2]

Today, by contrast, we welcome change and boast the ability to improve ourselves through psychological techniques without benefit of religious conversion. So, when is change good and when is it bad? What changes can I make in my life and what changes can be made only by God?

Confusion is compounded because some Christians claim that conversion is not ever needed by many people. They may concede that the experience is valid on the mission field where a drastic turnabout is required to renounce paganism—much like the situation in the New Testament. But in a "Christian nation" where religion is a pervasive influence, children who are nurtured in the faith from birth hardly need a conversion experience. The godly preacher, Phillips Brooks, who became an Episcopal bishop, once confessed that he did not know what conversion meant because he had never had a moment of identifiable crisis in his spiritual life.[3] Many people find it difficult to "convert" to Christianity when that is the only religion they have ever known.

Clearly we need to do more than commend conversion in idealistic terms as a cure-all for every human problem. Instead, we need to specify just *what* is changed by salvation, *when* it is changed, and *how much* it is changed. Is this change of which we speak sudden or gradual? partial or total? inward or outward? Do the same changes take place in every Christian's life, or do they vary between individuals? Do they take place to the same degree, or more in some than in others? Do they occur only at the outset of salvation, or do they continue to occur throughout life? Only as we answer questions such as these can we claim neither too little nor too much for the Christian experience of conversion.

Converted Lives in an Unconverted World

Christianity arose among groups with diametrically different conceptions of religious change. On the one hand, many Greek and Roman philosophers were skeptical that human nature could ever change. The Roman Stoic Seneca, for example, believed so deeply in total depravity that his sad conclusion was, "Wicked we are, wicked we have been, and, I regret to add, wicked we always will be."[4] On the other hand, many Jewish apocalypticists cherished the hope that the entire created order and its inhabitants would be suddenly and catastrophically transformed, resulting in the instant perfecting of those favored by God. For example, the book of Enoch, a non-biblical book, is full of descriptions of how the righteous will be blessed and shine with the brightness of the morning sun (58:2-6).

Christianity did not opt for either of these extremes. Instead of embracing the pessimistic view that nothing is ever going to change or the optimistic view that everything is soon going to change, it dared to assert the paradoxical view that human nature can be converted in the midst of an unconverted world. Whenever and wherever faith is open to the divine working of the Holy Spirit, then and there a process of radical change begins to occur. Eventually God is going to renovate the entire universe, but He is going to start by establishing a beachhead in each individual life. Between the beginning of the process of salvation and the ending, the Christian lives, as it were, in two worlds or, as Paul put it, "where the ages overlap" (1 Cor. 10:11, author's translation).

The process of conversion-in-the-midst-of-the-unconverted was worked out with care by the apostle Paul in Romans 5—8. At the outset, he placed the Christian in an environment influenced both by Adam, the ultimate source of all our problems, and by Christ, the ultimate source of all our answers (5:12-21). In the new world created by our spiritual dependence on Christ, we have died to sin and thus cut ourselves free from its clutches (6:1-11). However, in the old world sustained by our physical dependence on Adam, we must continue to resist sin as a tyrant seeking to reign in our mortal bodies (6:12-23). As children of Christ, we are already free from the tyranny of the law (7:1-12); but as children of Adam, we are still tormented by its uncompromising demands (vv. 13-25). In the new age of Christ, we are free from death to live by the Spirit (8:1-17); but in the old age of Adam, we still suffer and groan and are "being killed all the day long" (8:18-39).

The duality that is characteristic of all these teachings is occasioned by the fact that substantial changes begin to occur within the lives of Christians before any significant alterations begin to take place in the framework of their existence. The "Spirit of life" (Rom. 8:2) coexists in the "body of death" (7:24), and conversion takes place in the creative tension between the two! This relationship may be described as a tension between the indicative which declares that salvation is already available in Jesus Christ and the imperative which insists that we must appropriate it for ourselves. In Ephesians 4:22-24, for example, Christians are urged both to "put off your old nature" (v. 22) and to "put on the new nature" (v. 24). But this plea is possible only because we possess at the same time both an old nature "corrupt through deceitful lusts" (v. 22) and a new nature "created after the likeness of God" (v. 24).

To summarize: We live simultaneously in two distinct spheres. They may be called "life in the flesh" and "life in the spirit" or "the old nature" and "the new nature," but behind such descriptive terms lies a more basic reality. At bottom, one sphere is the realm of human existence organized around Christ and the other is the realm of human existence organized apart from Christ. That the Christian must inhabit both was signaled by Paul at the beginning of his letters. For example, in the first verse of Philippians "the saints" are described as being both "in Christ" and "in Philippi" (GNB; the RSV has "*at* Philippi" but the Greek preposition is the same). In other words, they were Christ-filled persons living in a sin-filled world. Life had two orientations; it breathed two atmospheres; it interacted with two competing pressures.

What this means for our understanding of conversion is that everything about life that is "in Christ" is being changed for the better by His indwelling presence, whereas everything about life that is "in Philippi," or wherever we live, is not necessarily changing for the better because it may be a realm where Christ is unknown or even opposed. And yet we are profoundly shaped by both spheres! Therefore, let me spell out the negative and positive implications of this dual citizenship for our experience of conversion.

What Conversion Does Not Change

No writings in all of religious history are more invincibly confident about the possibilities of human transformation than the New Testament, yet its pages are full of sober warnings which reflect a realistic awareness of what conversion does *not* change during this earthly life. Unless we face these limitations squarely, we may become presumptuous in supposing that we have been totally transformed and, therefore, overconfident in dealing with areas of life that need further change. Since it is from sin that we are to be saved (see Matt. 1:21), let us look at the effects of sin that are not changed by conversion. Once again, we may do this in relation to the three tenses of human experience.

The Results of Sin in the Past

No matter how soon we turn to God, all of us are keenly aware of sin in our lives both before and after the conversion experience. Writing to Christians, the apostle Paul made clear that, even for them, sin bears its bitter harvest: "Do not be deceived; God is not mocked, for whatever a man sows, that he will also reap" (Gal. 6:7). Examples are legion. If a person becomes addicted to alcohol prior to conversion, the body may still crave that drug long after the heart has changed. In like manner, many converted chain smokers still want a cigarette and many converted gluttons still want to overeat. Nor are the temptations only physical. Many a converted racist must still fight prejudice, and many a converted introvert must still struggle with loneliness. Nor are the implications limited only to ourselves. Irresponsible parents may contract venereal disease due to sexual sin and then be forgiven, but this change does not eradicate the transmitted infection which may cause their baby to become blind.

What these illustrations suggest is that acts have consequences. Once a cause-and-effect chain reaction is set in motion and becomes a part of the ongoing historical process, it cannot somehow be reversed or ignored as if it had not happened. Most people carry a number of acquired liabilities with them into the Christian faith: unproductive habits, unnatural dependencies, unhealthy relationships. Nor do they disappear the hour we first believe. Even *after* we are converted—in fact, precisely *because* we are converted—we may spend a lifetime disentangling ourselves from the unwanted legacy of the past. Nor is this only a matter of blame and punishment, for in many cases the inherited problem is not of our own making. At the time of conversion, we may be living with family members who are hostile to our new commitment or we may be working at a job which limits our Christian witness, due in large part to circumstances beyond our control.

Milton Eisenhower reminded us of the modern story of loving parents with a prodigal son. After the boy had dishonored his heritage, he returned home seeking a new relationship with his father. As they reviewed the past, the father confessed that his son's follies had wounded him like driving a stake into his heart, which he illustrated by hammering nail after nail into a nearby door as he recounted each indiscretion. Then, as the boy begged to be pardoned, his father mercifully consented, once again dramatizing his pledge by prying each nail out of the door with the hammer as he assured his son that the sin which it represented was henceforth forgiven. Finally, when the last nail had been pulled and discarded, the father said to his son, "I am so glad that you have come home and changed the way of life that hurt me so deeply. All of the nails driven into the door have now been removed, but the holes which they made in the wood will always remain. Just so, the ugly deeds that wounded my heart are all forgiven but I will carry the scars which they made for the rest of my life."[5]

In a very real sense, that story mirrors the meaning of conversion. Genuine change comes when our sins are forgiven as realistically as nails being removed from a door. But the holes the nails made still remain! That is, the sting of sin is drawn but its results endure. No matter how completely the penalty of sin is canceled, its consequences cannot be ignored. *Conversion does not mean that life can be lived as if the past never happened.* We shall reap what we sow, and even conversion will not cause a crop failure!

The Reality of Sin in the Present

Many churchgoers who hear the gospel week after week are lulled into an overconfident attitude toward sin. For the story of Jesus is often presented as if it were a simple matter for Him to defeat our sin. There are two things wrong with such an impression. First, the New Testament makes clear that Jesus' victory over sin was far from easy. In fact, by the end of His ministry the struggle had reached a level of desperate anguish unknown in human experience (Mark 14:33-36; John 12:27; Heb. 5:7-9). Second, we are far from being like Jesus. Even with His help in our lives, we cannot possibly mobilize the unique spiritual resources which enabled Him to become victorious over sin. *Conversion does not bestow perfection!* It neither makes us immune to sin nor does it insulate us from its seductiveness. "If we say we have no sin, we deceive ourselves, and the truth is not in us" (1 John 1:8).

The apostle Paul pinpointed our vulnerability to sin by explaining that, even though we have already been converted, we still live "in the *flesh*" (see for example, Rom. 8:3-8). By this he did not mean that our carnal nature is inherently evil and, therefore, the cause of sin in our lives. Rather, he meant that as long as our bodies are physical they are finite and that this mortality is a prime source of spiritual insecurity. In a futile effort to overcome our earthly limitations and combat the inevitability of death, we try either to pamper the flesh by indulging in forbidden pleasures or to glory in the flesh by boasting of our own accomplishments. But the physical is always temporary, and, if we cling to it as the only reality in life, we will sin against those realities which are unseen but eternal (see 2 Cor. 4:16-18).

The Risk of Sin in the Future

An outsider looking in on the Christian movement might suppose that its teachings become easier to live as discipleship matures. But history's greatest saints have testified that, if anything, the consciousness of sin becomes stronger as one's faith grows. After a great missionary career,

Adoniram Judson was heard to say as he lay dying, "I known I am a miserable sinner in the sight of God."[6] It seems that Satan reserves his fiercest temptations for those serious converts who can hurt his cause, while he feels safe to leave the indifferent Christian alone. To be sure, moral growth may free us from some of the grosser sins of the flesh that trouble the immature, but that achievement only shifts the battleground to those more subtle sins of the spirit that perplex even a silver-haired saint. *It is folly to suppose that in this life we will ever outgrow the threat of sin!*

This warning is not based on some theory but on the plain facts of Christian experience. The New Testament is full of those who, like Judas, failed at the finish (Luke 22:3-6) or, like Demas, forsook their earlier commitments (2 Tim. 4:10, 16). Our churches today are full of members whose growth is arrested, whose witness is hidden, whose usefulness is shattered by sin. According to their own testimony, they experienced what they understood to be a genuine conversion, but that in itself was no guarantee of victory over sin. Their lives warn us to set realistic expectations of what conversion can and does actually accomplish. To that positive consideration we now turn.

What Conversion Does Change

At first it might seem that in the previous section so many severe limitations were set on what conversion does *not* change that very little of importance is left for it *to* change. But God has chosen the really crucial areas of life on which to work His divine transformation even if these are viewed as insignificant by the world. Acts 26:18 well summarizes the positive side of conversion by describing it in terms of the inward, upward, and outward dimensions of our existence. In other words, God concentrates on transforming the central *relationships* of life: (1) Our relationship to *self*—"to open their eyes, that they may turn from darkness to light"; (2) Our relationship to *God*—"and from the power of Satan to God, that they may receive forgiveness of sins"; (3) Our relationship to *others*—"and a place among those who are sanctified by faith in [Christ]." Let us now explore each of these aspects of conversion.

In Relation to Self: A New Perspective

When our eyes are closed, everything is darkness no matter which direction we turn. But once our eyes have been opened, we may "turn from darkness to light" (Acts 26:18); that is, we gain a fresh angle of vision, a different orientation, a new perspective. Circumstances may not change, but now we are able to view those circumstances in an entirely new light. Because of the gift of spiritual insight, we are now free to face a new horizon, to choose a new direction, to reorder our priorities, and thereby to adopt a new hierarchy of values. Closed eyes symbolize a closed life: "If your eye is not sound, your whole body will be full of darkness" (Matt. 6:23). Conversely, open eyes symbolize an open life: "If your eye is sound, your whole body will be full of light" (v. 22). Conversion takes off the blindfold, throws open the shutters, and whets what Admiral Byrd called our "appetite for light."

Darkness distorts reality. As long as we "walk in darkness" (1 John 1:6), either because our eyes are closed or because it is night, we cannot discern what may be hidden by the blackness. Light, by contrast, discloses reality. When we "walk in the light" (v. 7), both because our eyes have been opened and because we now face the sunrise, we are able to see things as they really are. Conversion makes us sensitive to the whole realm of spiritual reality. Now we are able to choose a pathway without groping or stumbling in the dark. By turning us toward the light, conversion forever alters the whole bent of life.

In Relation to God: A New Power

Ultimately, there are just two kinds of power in this world, destructive and constructive. The "power of Satan" (Acts 26:18) is destructive. It seeks to corrupt, to enslave, and eventually to destroy. The power of God, by contrast, is constructive. It seeks to forgive, to liberate, and to develop. Conversion is a change of masters by which we are delivered from the tyranny of Satan and accepted by the grace of God. Through the Holy Spirit, a new power comes to dwell in our lives mightier than the power of Satan. Now we gain new desires, new affections, new motivations. From deep within, we are prompted not to hate but to love, not to hurt but to help, not to grasp but to give.

While it is true that we are not free from the *presence* of sin in our lives, we are freed by Christ from the *power* of sin to enslave. Infused with the divine dynamic of the Holy Spirit, we are no longer engaged in a losing battle with evil but are free to resist, to struggle, and even to prevail in the fight against sin. Released from the crushing load of guilt, we are no longer beaten, helpless, defeated slaves of sin. To be sure, sin can still tempt and seduce, but it can no longer dominate and destroy. The war is not over but the enemy is now on the defensive! Satan may counterattack in strength but, with Christ on our side, Satan is always repulsed by a superior force.

In Relation to Others: A New People

This does not mean, however, that we battle alone with only Christ at our side. As Acts 26:18 puts it, we are given "a place among those who are sanctified by faith." Baptism links us not only to our Lord but the army of His followers, the church. Here we find fellowship, an interlocking of life at the level of shared love. This network of supporters offers us instruction, inspiration, and example in what it means to be converted. Even when we fail, they restore us through a ministry of encouragement (Gal. 6:1). When we are weak, the strong rush to our rescue so that, when we are strong, we may "Bear one another's burdens" (Gal. 6:2).

Today, as never before, we realize the importance of peer pressure. In one sense, God's people are our peers who pressure us with the gentle persuasion of love to live by the faith which we share in common with them. In the company of the committed, we find our true selves for the first time. We also find Christ working in the power of His Spirit to energize the body. With fresh strength from within, from above, and from without, life slowly but surely begins to turn in a decisively new direction. Over a lifetime, we discover that, despite our failings, we are truly being converted!

Notes

1. William Barclay, *Turning to God: A Study of Conversion in the Book of Acts and Today* (Grand Rapids: Baker Book House, 1972, reprint), p. 13.

2. Henry F. Lyte, "Abide with Me," stanza 2.

3. Barclay, p. 94, citing W. R. Bowie, *Men of Fire*, p. 181.

4. Seneca, *On Benefits*, 1:10:2, 3, cited by Barclay, p. 12.

5. Milton S. Eisenhower, baccalaureate address, Pennsylvania State University, May 27, 1956.

6. Cited by Raymond E. Balcomb, "On Being Saved from Sin," *Church Management*, May 1952, p. 66.

Bibliography

Barclay, William. *Turning to God: A Study of Conversion in the Book of Acts and Today.* London: Epworth Press, 1963. 103 pages. Reprint: Grand Rapids: Baker Book House, 1972. 103 pages.

Conn, Walter E., editor. *Conversion: Perspectives on Personal and Social Transformation*. New York: Alba House, 1978. 330 pages.

Griffin, Emilie. *Turning: Reflections on the Experience of Conversion*. Garden City, N.Y.: Doubleday, 1980. 189 pages.

Harris, Irving, editor. *He Touched Me*. Nashville: Abingdon Press, 1985. 156 pages.

Jones, E. Stanley. *Conversion*. New York: Abingdon Press, 1959. 253 pages.

Kerr, Hugh T. and John M. Mulder, editors. *Conversions: The Christian Experience*. Grand Rapids: William B. Eerdmans Publishing Company, 1983. 265 pages.

Morris, George E. *The Mystery and Meaning of Christian Conversion*. Nashville: Disciple Resources, 1981. 194 pages.

Part III
The Consequences

We have been considering how salvation happens in human life. Our central finding is that it results from the interaction of human choice and divine change. From the human side, we respond to the offer of deliverance through repentance, faith, and confession. From the divine side, God responds to our willingness to be transformed by offering us regeneration, adoption, and conversion. The two movements, that of our lives to God and of God's life to us, finally become inseparable. Salvation is like marriage in that Savior and saved "become one" spiritually just as surely as bride and groom "become one" physically (Eph. 5:21-33). Just as a piece of paper cannot have only one side but must, by its very nature, have two, so salvation always has two sides as well, our upreach to God and His downreach to us.

Having clarified this dynamic balance, we are now ready to ask what salvation produces in the lives of those who embrace it. Granted that a divine-human relationship is established through the process of choosing described as repentance-faith-confession and the process of changing described as regeneration-adoption-conversion, what is the fruit of such a union? A search of Scripture reveals an emphasis on four consequences of a saving relationship to Jesus Christ: (1) forgiveness, (2) justification, (3) redemption, and (4) reconciliation. As is true of salvation itself, one's experience of these four realities commences at the outset of the Christian life, it continues to be deepened and enriched throughout the pilgrimage of discipleship, and it is completed in eternity when the earthly journey is ended.

The apostle Paul is the Bible's climactic interpreter of all four of these concepts both in relation to their appearance elsewhere in Scripture and in relation to each other. As we study Paul's epistles, the descriptions of these experiences sound to our modern ears like technical theological terms, but they were drawn directly from daily life in the first century.

As we shall see in the four chapters to follow, to be forgiven meant the removal of a barrier, to be justified meant the acquittal of a defendant, to be redeemed meant the emancipation of a slave, and to be reconciled meant the unifying of the alienated. In other words, as originally used these four concepts did not refer to abstract doctrines but to concrete experiences with which Paul's readers were already familiar.

What Paul did, in essence, was to describe salvation in terms of four vivid "word-pictures." Paul's Master had depicted salvation in stories called parables, but he compressed its implications into images which symbolize spiritual reality. It is very important to grasp the significance of his strategy in using figures of speech which were already familiar in the secular sphere. Even unbelievers knew what it was like for a road-block to be removed, for an accused to be declared not guilty, for a slave to be given freedom, or for a runaway to return home. These experiences were the stuff of ordinary life. They were the surprising breakthroughs that common folk delighted to talk about precisely because they were such joyful exceptions to the hum-drum of life as it was usually lived.

But what unbelievers discovered from the gospel was that experiences such as these also provided clues to the way in which God works and, therefore, to the meaning of salvation. To be precise, the human experiences of forgiveness, justification, redemption, and reconciliation served as *analogies* to the kinds of things that happen to those who are being saved. As such, they became bridges from the earthly to the eternal, from the physical to the spiritual, from the secular to the sacred. Christianity did not coin a private terminology to describe invisible realities; instead, it began with certain human experiences and used this visible imagery as the point of contact to help anyone "see" how salvation works deep within the heart. In so doing, by keeping the gospel anchored in *experience* rather than in *speculation,* Paul helped to preserve it from the fatal heresy of gnosticism to which any religion of deliverance is so susceptible.

As you approach the four doctrines to be surveyed in Chapters 8-11, do not view them as ideas but as actions. Try to picture them in terms of the graphic images in which they are expressed. Imagine how these experiences must have felt to people living in the first century. Search for parallel experiences that still happen to people today. Once you grasp the root meaning of each doctrine you will be able to find a point of contact by which to interpret its reality to those about you who need to discover its truth for their lives.

8
Forgiveness

"Forgiveness is a beggar's refuge," said George Bernard Shaw, "we must pay our debts." Perhaps that is why Huxley bluntly announced, "There is no such thing as forgiveness."[1] Thus do some see forgiveness as a fatal weakness of the Christian faith. But others see it as the hallmark of the gospel rooted in an essential characteristic of God. Alexander Pope made forgiveness almost axiomatic with his familiar aphorism, "To err is human, to forgive divine."[2] Or as Heinrich Heine quipped, probably echoing Voltaire, "God will pardon me: that's his business."[3]

These contradictory attitudes help to explain why forgiveness is one of the most misunderstood aspects of Christian salvation. Is it a moral fiction or a desperate necessity? Does it cheapen and corrupt the Christian doctrine of salvation or does it point us to the highest concept of salvation ever revealed to the human race? Does it permit us to turn back the calendar and live as if something sinful had not really happened, or does it actually wash clean Lady Macbeth's "spot"[4] and so purge the stain of an everlasting guilt?

To answer these controversial questions, we must first understand exactly what part forgiveness plays in the salvation process. Then we will be in a position to interpret both the divine role and the human role in the act of true forgiveness. We may start with a careful look at the way forgiveness functions in the Bible. You may be in for some surprises from this scriptural evidence because many sincere Christians have never grasped the central clue to the nature of forgiveness as set forth in God's Word.

The Meaning of Forgiveness

The Biblical Vocabulary

Just as there are several words to describe forgiveness in English, such as *pardon*, *remission*, and *reprieve*, so there are at least three main words for this reality in the Hebrew Old Testament and another three in the Greek New Testament. Taken together, they portray a cluster of concepts describing the nature of forgiveness in vivid images drawn from daily life. Let us begin by listing those concrete metaphors which are found most frequently in Scripture. There, forgiveness is depicted in the following terms:

(1) To carry off or send away something which is offensive by putting it either behind oneself or underfoot or in the depths of the sea (Ps. 103:3; Isa. 38:17; Mic. 7:19).

(2) To cover or conceal something by hiding it from sight, such as when forgetting or blotting out a painful memory (Ex. 29:36; Ps. 32:1; 1 Pet. 4:8).

(3) To cleanse or wipe away something by removing an ugly stain or washing off that which is defiled (Ps. 51:1,7; Isa. 43:25).

(4) To cancel an indebtedness by releasing someone from a binding obligation (Luke 6:37; 7:48).

(5) Not to count or impute a penalty by declining to enforce a judgment against someone deserving of punishment (Ps. 32:2; Acts 17:30).

(6) To care deeply for someone in difficulty by being gracious, displaying generosity, showing mercy (Luke 7:43; Eph. 4:32).

Despite its diversity, this vocabulary has one thing in common, namely, it describes *the removal of some hindrance to an effective relationship*. In other words, forgiveness is not an abstract theory but a decisive action whereby barriers between people are set aside. With that understanding in mind, let us now examine more closely how this transformation takes place.

The Biblical Syntax

When we examine the grammatical usage of the special words for forgiveness in Scripture, the key insight comes by grasping the way in which the action of removal is related to that which is removed. The latter is usually described in such terms as "sins, trespasses, blasphemies, and debts." A typical construction makes sins the direct object, and sinners the indirect object, of the verb for forgiveness. A literal translation would be: "God forgives in relation to us (dative case) our sins (accusative case)." What this means, quite simply, is that God does not "forgive" people or penalties; rather, He "forgives" sin, the root problem which caused difficulty in the first place. What is carried off or concealed or cleansed or canceled is sin itself. Contrary to the popular impression, forgiveness is not the way that God deals with us; rather, it is the way in which He deals with the transgressions that have separated us from Him.

Underlying this usage is the biblical assumption that sin is an objective reality, an independent entity that exists beyond our inner feelings. Sin is a concrete barrier, an obstacle, an impediment, an offense standing in the way of an unhindered relationship with God. "But your iniquities have made a separation between you and your God, and your sins have hid his face from you, so that he does not hear" (Isa. 59:2). To return to the images lurking in the vocabulary of forgiveness, sin is like a roadblock to be removed, an ugly abomination to be hidden, a pollution to be scrubbed clean. That is why sin creates distance, alienation, estrangement between God and the sinner. When people sin, they do not just break some impersonal rule. Instead, they succumb to a power with a life of its own that has the potency to impede and corrupt and finally frustrate true fellowship with God.

The Biblical Definition

Since sin, once it is committed, becomes a hideous thing between us and God, an act is required to remove it, that is, someone must do something to hide, cleanse, or banish it. We often think of sin as a bad attitude on our part toward God and of forgiveness as a good attitude on God's part toward us. But forgiveness is more than an attitude. It is an action, a struggle, a divine deed in the drama of salvation. It is not God "letting us off free" as a moral fiction, but God working to alter a situation, break an impasse, resolve a stalemate, overcome an obstacle. According to the Bible, *forgiveness is God doing whatever it takes to remove every hindrance to fellowship created by our sin*.

The result, therefore, of divine intervention *by* God is that a new way is opened for us *to* God. Once we are forgiven, we are not necessarily any better in a moral sense, and certainly are far from perfect; but we do gain an access to God which was formerly blocked by our sin. The gospel of forgiveness announces a new opportunity, an altered situation of openness and availability because barriers which we could not penetrate have been dismantled by God. As stressed in the previous chapter, the consequences of sin are not suspended, as if the laws of cause and effect no longer functioned. But now we can cope with these penalties in the strength of God's power because sin no longer blocks the way.

The Divine Role in Forgiveness

The Character of God

Since the task of forgiveness is to deal decisively with the threat of sin, then God must do the forgiving, for we are victims of sin's power and therefore unable to overcome its curse. Only He can remove our transgressions from us "as far as the east is from the west" (Ps. 103:12). Ultimately, forgiveness is *from* God as its source, *by* God as its agent, and *for* God as its goal. This points to the deepest character of God as sheer grace. Divine love combines the freedom that allows us to sin with the righteousness that determines to remove the obstructions caused by sin.

God's character as forgiving stands in sharp contrast to the way in which pagan deities were understood in the ancient world. The wars that erupted almost constantly in the Near East were viewed as conflicts between competing gods, with total victory over the enemy as a primary objective in the struggle. For one deity to pardon another was unthinkable. In paganism, the gods fought to annihilate their competitors, not to forgive them! Against that backdrop, consider how revolutionary was the teaching of Jesus that we are to love even our enemies because that is precisely what God does (Matt. 5:44-45). For God to "grace" His enemies with forgiveness represented a radically new departure from the pagan idea of deity as one who visited vengeance on every foe.

A remarkable expression of this grace is conveyed by the Old Testament concept of God "forgetting" our iniquities. " I, I am He who blots out your transgressions for my sake, and I will not remember your sins" (Isa. 43:25; compare Jer. 31:34). In following the proverbial advice to "forgive and forget," we usually find the latter more difficult to do than the former. Yet God the omniscient One is willing to practice a kind of deliberate "divine amnesia" on our behalf. Consistent with what I said about God forgiving sin rather than the sinner, this does not mean that He fails to remember *us* but rather that He blots out any memory of our misdeeds.

The High Cost of Forgiveness

As incredible as it may sound for an all-knowing God to "forget" anything, especially our transgressions against Him, we nevertheless are tempted to assume that forgetting is a relatively easy thing for God to do because it only involves dismissing some memory from the mind. But forgiveness is infinitely costly to God because it involved the sending of His Son to die on the cross. Paul connected most of the dimensions of forgiveness that have been discussed to this point in Colossians 2:13-14. "And you, who were dead in trespasses . . . God made alive together with him, having forgiven us all our trespasses, having canceled the bond which stood against us with its legal demands; this he set aside, nailing it to the cross."

Throughout His earthly ministry, Jesus incarnated the forgiveness of God in the commonplace circumstances of life. By His parables, He taught the limitlessness of forgiveness (Luke 7:36-50). By His miracles, He acted out the liberating power of forgiveness (Mark 2:1-12). By eating with sinners, He dramatized God's acceptance of those who had been ostracized from religious circles because of their reputations (Mark 2:13-17; Luke 15:1-2). Finally, on the cross, He forgave the cruelest enemies God had ever known (Luke 23:34). Jesus did not die in order that He could forgive sin, as is sometimes said; rather, He died because He had already been forgiving sin throughout His earthly ministry.

Mediators of Forgiveness

In the Judaism of Jesus' day, forgiveness was often seen as something that God would do to banish sin at the end of time in heaven. Until then, the sacrificial system here on earth foreshadowed that future victory (Heb. 10:1-4). But Jesus brought the divine pardon "down to earth," daring to announce that sins could be forgiven in the here and now entirely apart from the Temple and priesthood. To the Jewish theologians ("scribes") of that day, the notion that an untrained, unauthorized layman could offer forgiveness to anyone was blasphemous (Mark 2:5-7)! But the common people readily grasped the point and glorified God that He "had given such authority *to men*" (Matt. 9:8, author's italics). No longer was the procedure for obtaining forgiveness remote and institutional; now it was immediate and personal.

In this spirit, Jesus delegated to His followers the authority to forgive sins in His name. This is the meaning of the unusual promise in Matthew 16:19, "I will give you the keys of the kingdom of heaven, and whatever you bind on earth shall be bound in heaven, and whatever you loose on earth shall be loosed in heaven." The ancient Jewish concept of "binding" and "loosing" is explained in the parallel promise of John 20:23, "If you forgive [that is, "loose"] the sins of any, they are forgiven; if you retain [that is, "bind"] the sins of any, they are retained." What this means for us today is that when we bear witness to the gospel of Jesus Christ, we are authorized to assure our hearers that their sins are forgiven here and now if only they will respond to the finished work of Christ in faith.

The Human Role in Forgiveness

Since only God can remove our sins so far away that even He forgets them, are we entirely passive in the process? Not at all! Even when our sinful situation has been altered so that we have access to God, we must avail ourselves of that new opportunity in order for it to become meaningful in our lives. In so doing, we activate the whole range of responses to God's salvation already surveyed in the early chapters of this book. Here I will mention three which are emphasized in Scripture.

Repentance

Repentance is regularly associated with forgiveness in the Bible, as we can tell from the preaching of John the Baptist (Mark 1:4), Jesus (Luke 17:3-4), and Peter at Pentecost (Acts 2:38). Why should this be so? Because if God comes when we expect it least to remove every hindrance created by sin, we will not even realize that the barriers are down unless we are looking in the right direction. The "about-face" which takes place in repentance allows us to see for the first time that the roadblocks which sent us on a detour have been removed and a new way opened to God.

Confession

The Bible also makes a close connection between forgiveness and confession. "If we *confess* our sins, He is faithful and just, and will *forgive* our sins and cleanse us from all unrighteousness" (1 John 1:9, author's italics). Baptism is the definitive expression of that confession of faith, which explains why it is linked both to repentance and to forgiveness (Mark 1:4-5; Acts 2:38). In confession we acknowledge both that we cannot remove our own sin and that Christ has done it for us. This open recognition of reality is our first step toward claiming the promise of Christ's cleansing work, that is, we will only *act* on that which we are first willing to *admit* is true!

Forgiveness of Others

Finally, we are to forgive others if we want forgiveness for ourselves (Matt. 6:12). This is the one petition in the Lord's Prayer singled out for emphasis in the commentary which follows (Matt. 6:14-15). In the ancient world, only a subservient person begged forgiveness; but for Jesus the strong or innocent party initiated such an appeal (Matt. 5:23-24). Why did Jesus suggest so radical a change? Because to forgive was to be like God (Luke 6:36)! By contrast, "to be unforgiving is to remain unforgiven because one is thus unforgiveable."[5]

Now we are able to address the issue of forgiveness as a "beggar's paradise" raised by George Bernard Shaw. We have seen that forgiveness does not pretend to make us morally perfect; rather, it changes the terms of our dealings with God by removing the hindrances caused by sin. But in so doing, it calls us to become not only *forgiven* but also *forgivers:* barrier breakers, garbage collectors, decontamination agents of the poisons that cause human relations to fester. To be sure, we cannot change others any more than we can change ourselves. But in the spirit of Christ, we can alter the climate, remove the impediments, and create the openness in which healing can take place. A forgiveness powerful enough to make us forgiving is not a moral fiction!

Part III began with a chapter on forgiveness because this is the way in which God deals decisively with our *sin* as the foundation for changing the *sinner*. In our modern preoccupation with inner feelings, we like to think that every problem will be solved if only attitudes and relationships are altered. But often this proves impossible to achieve until the polluted atmosphere in which those relationships exist has first been purified. It is not a pleasant task to lug off a lot of garbage dumped by envy, malice, and strife. But cleaning up what is *between* people is prerequisite to bringing people together. Christ can reunite us both to God and to one another because He is "the Lamb of God, who *takes away* the sin of the world!" (John 1:29, author's italics).

Notes

1. Both quotations are cited in James S. Stewart, *A Faith to Proclaim* (London: Hodder and Stoughton, 1953), p. 65.

2. Alexander Pope, *Essay on Criticism*, part II, line 15. Cited in John Bartlett, *Familiar Quotations*, fifteenth edition (Boston: Little, Brown, 1955), p. 33.

3. Cited in Frank S. Mead, editor, *The Encyclopedia of Religious Quotations* (Westwood, N.J.: Fleming H. Revell, 1965), p. 147.

4. William Shakespeare, *Macbeth*, act V, scene 1, line 33.

5. Frank Stagg, *New Testament Theology* (Nashville: Broadman, 1962), p. 92.

Bibliography

Ashcraft, Jesse Morris. *The Forgiveness of Sins*. Nashville: Broadman Press, 1972. 128 pages.

Emerson, Jr., James Gordon. *The Dynamics of Forgiveness*. Philadelphia: Westminster Press, 1964. 203 pages.

Klassen, William. *The Forgiving Community*. Philadelphia: Westminster Press, 1966. 253 pages.

Redlich, E. Basil. *The Forgiveness of Sins*. Edinburgh: T. & T. Clark, 1937. 339 pages.

Taylor, Vincent. *Forgiveness and Reconciliation: A Study in New Testament Theology*. London: Macmillan, 1941. 288 pages.

9

Justification

One of the most gripping dramas in human experience is a courtroom trial. The interplay between plaintiff and defendant, lawyers and witnesses, judge and jury, is for us the very essence of conflict and resolution. And what is the climax of this judicial process? The verdict! That is why we rivet attention on even a tedious lawsuit: Everything hinges on the judgment rendered. From the very first moment, suspense builds in response to the one unanswered question that dominates the entire proceeding: innocent or guilty?

Beyond our interest in whatever issues may come before the bar of justice, we find the courtroom endlessly fascinating because it symbolizes for us the essential character of life as one long litigation in which each of us is on trial. We go to school for years, hoping that our record will admit us to the college of our choice. But will we be accepted? We work for years at a job, wondering if our performance will entitle us to promotion. We spend years raising our children, then hold our breath to see if they will "turn out all right" in adulthood. We are forever being accused and defended, indicted and exonerated, censured and commended. And through this endless examination, we cannot help but wonder what the final verdict will be on how we have lived our lives.

Nor can we escape that eventual assessment. If nothing else, death itself draws a bottom line and demands an ultimate accounting. For beyond death looms eternity and the judgment of God, not only on our earthly past but on our future destiny as well. When all is said and done, will the Great Judge answer yes or no to us? The biblical teaching on justification is designed to deal with this supreme question in life. This doctrine does more than explain how God goes about evaluating our lives. More importantly, it enables us to know *now* what the final verdict will be that determines our standing in God's sight. In the preaching of the gospel, we are brought before the bar of heaven and, by our response, are declared acquitted or condemned for time and eternity.

"Justification by faith" was the great watchword of the Protestant Reformation which launched a new era in Christian history. On the lips of Martin Luther that truth became a trumpet call to overcome the perversions that had corrupted medieval Catholicism. But that was not the first time that "justification by faith" had been used as a weapon of spiritual warfare. The apostle Paul also employed it in developing the doctrine to its highest biblical expression in his controversies with Judaism. In fact, the best way to understand this dimension of the salvation experience is to examine it in the light of three sharp contrasts, drawn out most fully in Galatians and Romans, between the way justification was viewed in the Judaism from which Paul came and the Christianity to which he was converted.

Law or Grace?

In Galatians 2:15-21, Paul translated autobiography into theology by reminding Peter of the profound difference between their pre-Christian lives as Jews and their subsequent lives as Christians. In the former status they sought to be justified "by works of law" but found that endeavor to be impossible. Instead, they discovered that they could be justified "by faith in Jesus Christ" (v. 16). From the before-and-after experience of frustration and fulfillment, Paul developed a clear distinction between justification based on "the law" and justification based on "the grace of God" (v. 21). What are the differences between these two approaches to salvation?

Law in Judaism

We usually think of law in civil or criminal categories, but in Judaism it was a deeply spiritual reality (Rom. 2:14). Nor did it have the negative meanings which we often assign to the term *legalism*. Beginning in the Old Testament, law *(Torah)* referred to the revelation of God's will for the whole of life, not to a code regulating the practice of religion. The law was a guideline for the people of God which defined how they could be faithful to the divine convenant. In that sense, Paul could speak of the law in positive terms as "holy and just and good" (Rom. 7:12).

In revealing God's will, however, the law also revealed the failure of God's people to keep His will. In that sense Paul could say, "through the law comes knowledge of sin" (Rom. 3:20). Ironically, by exposing sin for what it really is, the law drives a religious person to try even harder to follow God's will, but that effort inevitably fails because "all have sinned" (v. 23). A vicious cycle develops according to which a person tries harder and harder to obey the law, even to the point of becoming a religious fanatic (Phil. 3:6), but that only intensifies a sense of frustration resulting in anguished wretchedness (Rom. 7:24).

To say that sinful passions are "aroused by the law" (Rom. 7:5) does not mean, of course, that the law itself "is sin" (v. 7). But because it goads us to efforts which cause us to sin (v. 5), the law is in that sense a curse (Gal. 3:10-13). Therefore, the only way to be free of its power to provoke us to sin is to cease completely from any dependence on the law as the basis for our standing before God. That is what Paul meant when he declared that Christians have "died to the law" (Gal. 2:19) in order to escape its binding obligations, just as a married woman is "discharged from the law concerning her husband" should he die (Rom. 7:1-4). This illustration does not imply that Christians are free to ignore God's will as revealed by the law. Rather, Paul was insisting that we can never make ourselves acceptable to God by virtue of the way in which we keep His law (Rom. 3:20; Gal. 2:16). The law is indispensable as a guide to human conduct but inadequate as a source of divine acceptance.

Grace in Christianity

In contrast to the futility of our feverish efforts to be justified through obedience to the law, Paul asserted that Jews and Gentiles alike "are justified by [God's] grace as a gift" (Rom. 3:24). "Grace" means God's favor freely bestowed on the undeserving. In the Old Testament, God had graciously given the law through Moses (John 1:17) to the most insignificant people on earth. But then He sent His only Son so that all who believe might be "justified in Christ" (Gal. 2:17). We often use the familiar phrase "justification *by faith*" as if our faith were somehow the means of securing God's favor. A more accurate statement is that we are justified *by grace* through faith (compare Eph. 2:8), understanding *grace* to mean the gift of Jesus Christ Himself for our salvation.

The crucial point to stress is that we are not so much justified *by faith* as we are justified *by Christ!* In other words, the quality of *our* faith does not make us acceptable to God any more than does the quality of *our* works. Rather, the quality of what Jesus Christ has done *for us* makes all of the difference in God's sight. We usually contrast faith with works and assume that, for the Christian, works play no part since justification is entirely by faith. The more important contrast, however, is between *our* works, which are inadequate, and *Christ's* works, which are all-sufficient, in making us right with God. To be sure, our salvation is not based on *human* works (Eph. 2:9), but it is based directly on the *divine* work of Christ!

Paul made this very clear by rooting justification in the two climactic events of Jesus' earthly ministry. First, Christ died for our sins on the cross, which means that "we are now *justified by His blood*" (Rom. 5:9, author's italics). Earlier the apostle had said that we are justified by the gift of Christ Jesus "whom God put forward as an expiation by his blood" (Rom. 3:25). What that difficult language means is that the Father offered His own Son as a sacrifice for our sins. God allowed Christ to die as an innocent victim of the suffering which we deserve for our misdoings. But, in the second place, God "raised from the dead Jesus our Lord" (4:24), thereby vindicating Him "who was put to death for our trespasses and *raised for our justification*" (v. 25, author's italics).

Notice that both the sacrificial death of Christ and His victorious resurrection were gifts of God to us. We did absolutely nothing to help Christ die in perfect obedience and love—He did it all alone with only the help of God. Nor did we do anything to bring Christ from the tomb,—again, that was entirely an act of God. And yet both were acts of God for us—gifts that are utterly free if only we will have them. Which means that, finally, the only thing we can *offer to God* is that which has been provided *by God*. Standing before the bar of heaven, the only evidence we can present to the Great Judge of the universe in pleading our case is not the evidence of what we have done for Him (that is, the "works of law"), but the evidence of what He has done for us (that is, the finished work of Christ). The only reason we can offer such evidence to God is because He first offered it to us—with "no strings attached"—in the preaching of the gospel.

Works or Faith?

For Paul, there were two alternative sources of justification, the divine law given through Moses and the divine grace given through Jesus Christ. But each option called forth a distinctly different human response. Law, by its very nature, demands obedience, which is why "*works* of the law" became a standardized phrase in Paul. But grace, by its very nature, demands receptivity, which is why "*faith* in Jesus

Christ" became the contrasting phrase for Paul (for example, Gal. 2:16). Thus we have a second pair of options to examine as regards, not the source, but the means of justification: works versus faith. What is the difference between them?

Works in Judaism

Paul was well aware that the law of God laid a claim on conduct: "For it is not the *hearers* of the law who are righteous before God, but the *doers* of the law who will be justified" (Rom. 2:13, author's italics). He had personally experienced the motivation of the law so strongly that it had driven him to become a religious zealot (Gal. 1:14). Insofar as was humanly possible, Paul could claim that "as to righteousness under the law" he was "blameless" (Phil. 3:6). Much like the rich young ruler who came to Jesus, the Jewish Saul of Tarsus could say of the Commandments, "All these I have observed from my youth" (Mark 10:20). Far from being arrogant claims to perfection, these were the sincere testimonies of earnest Jews who took the law with great seriousness.

Then why are works insufficient as a means of justification? First, no matter how zealously they are performed, our works never meet all of the expectations of the law. "For all who rely on works of the law are under a curse; for it is written, 'Cursed be every one who does not *abide by all things* written in the book of the law, and do them'" (Gal. 3:10, author's italics). To break one law is to break the whole law, while to keep many laws does not excuse the neglect of a few laws. Second, works cannot justify because the ones which we do perform adequately give rise to a self-reliant attitude of boasting. Ephesians 2:9 explains clearly why salvation is not of works, "lest any man should *boast*" (compare Rom. 3:27; 4:2; 1 Cor. 1:29,31, author's italics). The fatal sin of pride always lurks close at hand to corrupt our best efforts to please God with good deeds.

Faith in Christianity

In contrast to works, faith is not an achievement but an attitude, not an activity of our own doing but a willingness to receive for ourselves that which is of God's doing. As such, faith is the opposite of boasting because it recognizes that our acquittal by God is something received rather than achieved. This does not mean, however, that faith is a matter of good fortune, as if justification were the result of a lucky draw, the unexpected payoff such as comes to the holder of a winning lottery ticket.

Instead, faith is a free and open surrender which anyone may offer to God, an abdication of autonomy, a willingness to let God have the last word rather than reserving the last word for ourselves. It is placing our lives at God's disposal in the confidence that He can do far more for us than we could ever do for ourselves.

Although ours is a "righteousness from God that *depends on faith*" (Phil. 3:9, author's italics), this does not mean faith is the source of justification. Faith is the *condition* of receiving grace but not the *cause* of it being offered, as if faith were some sort of work or merit by which we earn God's favor. Faith is not the *reason* some are justified while others are not, as if those with faith are thereby better than those without it. Rather, faith is the *response* by which we accept the acquittal of God offered to all. In summary, faith is an eagerness to let God give us Jesus Christ at the center of our beings and to relate to us as persons filled with the Spirit of His Son. That understanding of faith leads us to the last and greatest issue in Paul's dialogue with his Jewish past.

Godly or Ungodly?

In the background of this entire discussion of justification looms the courtroom as a stage on which is played out the drama of condemnation or acquittal. But that bar of justice in biblical times was quite different from courtrooms today. A modern trial is primarily a contest between competing attorneys before a jury. The scene is crowded with prosecutors and defenders, witnesses and spectators, bailiffs and clerks, all following complex procedures enforced by a judge. But in the ancient world, the scene was much simpler. A trial meant being brought summarily before the king or his representative and being accused of breaking the law. The sovereign questioned, the accused responded, and the verdict was rendered. Often in a split second issues of ultimate destiny were decided, for the king's word was law and his ruling was final. Justice was dispensed face to face; in that one-on-one encounter, everything depended on what the judge decreed.

Set against that background, the biblical concept of justification is based entirely on the judgment of God. It matters not at all what legal precedents might be cited or how skillfully the lawyers on either side might maneuver. Rather, in each person's lonely encounter with the Judge of the universe, the only thing that matters is the verdict which He announces. The dominant conviction of the entire Bible is that God always judges *rightly* because righteousness is His essential character.

Unlike earthly despots who might be fickle or even frivolous in their rulings, God can never be unpredictable or tyrannical because that would deny His very nature as a "righteous judge" (2 Tim. 4:8). Although the Old Testament and the New Testament are in complete agreement on this basic premise, at this point the deepest difference emerged in the Jewish and Christian understanding of justification.

Justification of the Godly in Judaism

Based on the conviction that God Himself is righteous, Judaism logically concluded that He could justify, or acquit as innocent, only those who are themselves righteous by obedience to divine law. After all, the Old Testament spoke frequently of the justification of the righteous in the sense of divine vindication of a godly life. Psalm 11 is typical:

> The Lord tests the righteous and the wicked,
> and his soul hates him that loves violence.
> For the Lord is righteous, he loves righteous deeds;
> the upright shall behold his face (vv. 5,7).

Paul himself accepted the premise that a righteous God cannot but abhor unrighteous behavior. In the "great indictment" of Romans 1:18 to 3:20, the apostle roundly condemned Jew and Gentile alike for presuming to think that they could escape the judgment of God that "rightly falls upon those" who sin (2:2). But that was precisely the problem because "*all* men, both Jews and Greeks, are under the power of sin" (3:9, author's italics), a conclusion which Paul supported by citing another side of the Old Testament testimony in Psalm 14:1, "None is righteous, no not one" (Rom. 3:10). Here, then, is the central dilemma posed for Christianity by the Jewish view of justification: If God justifies only the righteous because He Himself is righteous, how can He justify anyone, since every person is, in fact, unrighteous?

Justification of the Ungodly in Christianity

Paul responded to this dilemma with the deepest claim of the gospel: God "justifies the *ungodly*" (Rom. 4:5, author's italics). But how can this be? Does it not contradict everything the apostle said in Romans 1:18 to 3:20 about the wrath of God judging "all ungodliness and wickedness of men" (1:18; compare 2:5)? No, because Paul went on in this very passage to explain how *God can justify the unrighteous in such a way that it will make them righteous!* It is not that God simply declares us to be innocent when we are actually guilty, which would mean that His verdict is a moral fiction. Rather, he offers the gift of acquittal to all who have faith in Jesus Christ because those who accept these terms do in fact become righteous by virtue of the work of Christ in their lives.

The crux of this astonishing claim is to be found in Paul's use of a verb variously translated as to "impute" (KJV), "reckon" (RSV), or "count" (NEB, NIV). The word itself has three aspects. It means (1) to consider, estimate, or evaluate someone; (2) in order to attribute, ascribe, or allot something to them; (3) so that they can then be viewed, regarded, or looked upon in a different fashion. Paul used this term in two ways when speaking of those who stood before God with faith in Christ. Negatively, he claimed that God would not hold against them the sins which would otherwise lead to a verdict of guilty (Rom. 4:8; 2 Cor. 5:19). Positively, he claimed that God would take into account their faith as a legitimate basis for judging them to be righteous and so worthy of acquittal (Rom. 4:3-12,22-25; Gal. 3:6). Significantly, because Paul was departing so drastically from Judaism, he based both contentions squarely on the Old Testament, the former on Psalm 32:2 and the latter on Genesis 15:6.

For many sincere Jews and Christians, the notion of "imputed righteousness" is the most difficult aspect of the Pauline doctrine of justification to understand and accept. The protest of Vincent Taylor is often cited: "Since it is not a commodity, but a personal state, righteousness cannot be transferred from the account of one person to another. Righteousness can no more be imputed to a sinner than bravery to a coward or wisdom to a fool."[1] But God looks at us in the light of Christ's righteousness, not in the sense of a mechanical transfer from one independent life to another, but because Christ is "in us" and we are "in Him" as the result of an indivisible union which makes His the mind by which we think, the heart by which we feel, and the will by which we act. Put simply, Christ becomes our righteousness because, by faith, Christ becomes our life!

Paul expressed profoundly the principle of identification in 2 Corinthians 5:21. The verse speaks first of Christ's identification with our sin: "For our sake he [God] made him [Christ] to be sin who knew no sin." This does not mean that Jesus became a moral reprobate who committed evil acts; rather, it means that on the cross he gave Himself so completely to us in love that He experienced the full depth of our sinful predicament. The verse goes on to speak of our identification with Christ's righteousness: "that in him we might become the righteousness of God." This does not mean that we become morally perfect, any more than the first half of the verse means that Christ became morally evil. Rather, it means that we may give ourselves so completely to Christ in faith that we experience the reality of His righteousness energizing our lives and that God accepts that reality as the basis of our acquittal.

For centuries, justification has been described in legal categories, thereby making imputation a cold, argumentative term. But the reality which it seeks to describe is far more dynamic than this usage would imply. The righteousness of God is not so much a divine attribute as it is a divine activity by which God works to make things right. This He does by offering us Christ, the perfect embodiment of His own righteousness. If we are willing, by faith, to let the Spirit of Christ fill our very beings, then divine righteousness is at work in us as fact, not fiction. Now righteousness is ours because Christ is ours. When God looks at us, He sees the righteousness that comes through faith in Christ rather than the unrighteousness that comes from futile efforts to keep the law. A divine code, for all of its value, does not have the capacity to create righteousness in our lives as does a divine Companion.

Once God sees that we are willing for Christ to live at the center of our lives, He immediately declares us "justified," thereby enabling us to know for certain that what Christ is doing in us is totally acceptable to Him. Long before the process by which Christ makes our lives "right" is completed, we are guaranteed what the eventual outcome will be. The assurance precedes the achievement because we need the encouragement of God's approval to "press on" in the long journey to perfection (Phil. 3:12). Ultimately, therefore, justification is God's verdict on the significance of accepting Christ into our lives. It is the gift of an unshakable confidence that, because God has "found" us in Christ, we now have a righteousness not of our own doing, based on law, but a righteousness from God that comes through faith in Jesus Christ (v. 9).

Note

1. Vincent Taylor, *Forgiveness and Reconciliation: A Study in New Testament Theology* (London: Macmillan, 1946), p. 57.

Bibliography

Barth, Markus. *Justification: Pauline Texts Interpreted in the Light of the Old and New Testaments*. A. M. Woodruff, III, trans. Grand Rapids: Wm. B. Eerdmans, 1971. 90 pages.

Forde, Gerhard O. *Justification by Faith—A Matter of Death and Life*. Philadelphia: Fortress, 1982. 103 pages.

Kaesemann, Ernst. "'The Righteousness of God' in Paul," *New Testament Questions of Today* (Philadelphia: Fortress, 1969), pp. 168-182; "Justification and Salvation History in the Epistle to the Romans," *Perspectives on Paul* (Philadelphia: Fortress, 1971), pp. 60-78.

10
Redemption

As midnight approached on July 31, 1838, William Knibb gathered ten thousand slaves on the island of Jamaica to celebrate the Emancipation Act that would go into effect on the next day. An immense coffin was filled with whips, branding irons, handcuffs, and other symbols of servitude. At the first stroke of midnight, Knibb shouted, "The monster is *dying!*" At the final stroke he cried, "The monster is *dead!* Let us bury him!" They screwed the coffin shut, lowered it into a twelve-foot grave, and covered it over, thus burying forever the last vestiges of their hideous bondage. As with one voice, ten thousand hoarse throats shouted in praise of human freedom.[1]

That same sense of deliverance from oppression is a dominant note in the Christian experience of salvation. The New Testament reads like one long emancipation proclamation. On its pages one can hear the tolling of a new age in which the shackles of enslavement to evil are being snapped and the monster that has kept humanity in fetters is beginning to die. The single word *redemption* gathers up this joyful sense of liberation from captivity to sin. The term translates two Greek word families which mean (1) "to release from confinement," such as, in being set free from prison, and (2) "to ransom" or buy back, such as, in purchasing a slave's freedom. The many vivid images that cluster around this concept in Scripture suggest three things about the nature of salvation.

The Plight

Common to every situation with which redemption deals is a sense of powerlessness, even helplessness, a loss of self-determination, a feeling of being hemmed in by forces that stifle freedom. As the title of an autobiographical novel by W. Somerset Maugham described it, the condition which redemption addresses is one "of human bondage." To be sure, in this enlightened era when slavery has been banished from American life, very few think any longer of involuntary servitude as a symbol of human plight. Rather, what we struggle with today is a vague sense of claustrophobia, of living in cramped quarters, of being constricted by forces beyond our control.

Most of the time, however, the typical modern American feels no conscious sense of servitude. Many people have never thought of themselves as being trapped in prisons from which they need to escape. In fact, the modern mood conditions us to be confident and optimistic, to think that we can lick any problem. Our generation has been energized by new discoveries, bouyed by unprecedented prosperity, lulled into thinking that there are now almost no constraints on our freedom. To such a mindset, the suggestion that we need redemption is viewed as a cop-out at best, an insult at worst. This doctrine seems to make Christianity a religion for weaklings by promising that, to those who feel helpless and imprisoned, God will come and turn the key. Never in history have so many people been so intoxicated with a sense of self-determination. So we must ask: is redemption a crutch for those too insecure and dependent to help themselves?

By defining our plight in terms of powerlessness, the doctrine of redemption has become suspect to some as a put-down of human dignity and resourcefulness. Nor can we deny that many well-meaning Christians have allowed a gospel of divine deliverance to pamper their weaknesses and numb their sense of responsibility. But before we emancipate ourselves from the need to be emancipated by God, let us remember how often all of us have felt trapped, either by a past which we cannot change or by a future which we cannot predict. Eugene O'Neill described it poignantly at the personal level: "None of us can help the things life has done to us. They're done before you realize it, and once they're done, they make you do other things until at last everything comes between you and what you'd like to be, and you have lost your true self forever."[2]

Perhaps we can grasp the nature of our collective predicament by pondering the recent course of American history. In the fifties and early sixties we were flushed with the victories of World war II, heady with the scientific triumphs of nuclear energy and space travel, our cities exploding with prosperity and population. The baby boom was our vote of confidence in a future when we would cross a "New Frontier" and build a "Great Society" free of minority exploitation, of urban slums, of cold war strife. But then came ghetto uprisings, campus riots, political assassinations, the quagmire of Vietnam, the long nightmare of Watergate, the energy crunch, runaway inflation, and spiraling national debt—all of which we were helpless to prevent and unable to control. Despite our vaunted achievements, we, the most powerful nation on earth, were powerless to fulfill our dreams!

Whether viewed individually or collectively, our plight is paradoxical. On the one hand, we want to be responsible for winning our freedom and determining our destiny, and there is something noble about that desire. But, on the other hand, we are simply not able to achieve these goals in our own strength. Again and again we reach an impasse despite our well-meaning efforts. We think of Robert Oppenheimer struggling with the use of atomic power, of John F. Kennedy with the Bay of Pigs, of Robert McNamara with Vietnam, of Gerald Ford with the pardon of Nixon, of Jimmy Carter with the Iranian hostages, of Ronald Reagan with the national deficit and we see some of the most powerful leaders of our time trapped in a prison of circumstance from which they could not escape. At a more personal level, all of us desire inner freedom but finally despair of our ability to achieve it. Once we recognize the need for help, where is it to be found?

The Price

We must begin with a recognition that tyranny, while terrible for the victim, is highly advantageous for the tyrant. Landlords profit handsomely from those slums that we try to clean up. Businesses enjoy the cheap labor institutionalized by racial prejudice. Even war is an enormous boon to the victors who plunder the vanquished, to the armament manufacturers who win fat government contracts, and to the politicians who get credit for victories. All of which is to say that tyrants do not give up the advantages of their tyranny without a fight. When challenged to relinquish their stranglehold on the oppressed, as were the Egyptians by Moses, they demand a high price to compensate for their loss and, if it is not forthcoming, they fight tenaciously to keep what they have.

Even when we are our own worst enemy, when our bondage is to inheritance or insecurity or indulgence, we are still very reluctant to change. Challenge a man enslaved to alcohol to give up the bottle and watch him fight to keep that wretched habit. Challenge a woman who has always lived on the "wrong side of the tracks" to risk new relationships that will enlarge her experience and watch her cling to the security of her inherited class. It takes a tremendous "offer" to persuade us to trade the familiar for the unknown. It requires a huge inducement to melt the hardened heart, to prick the dulled conscience, to break out of well-worn ruts. Once we are entrenched in some chronic pattern of servitude, whether because of our own capitulation or because of external pressure, it is costly to effect a change.

This stubbornness of sin to yield any ground once it gains the upper hand explains why the notion of a price to be paid is at the heart of most pictures of redemption. In Old Testament times, the next of kin was responsible to come up with the funds necessary to buy back a family member from slavery or to satisfy an indebtedness against family property. In the case of an adversary who refused to negotiate, the price required was an exertion of strength necessary to break the grip of the tyrant. God adopted Israel as His people and so became their "next of kin" (Isa. 44:24; 47:4), the relative responsible to redeem them from captivity, not by paying an earthly ransom of silver (Isa. 45:13; 52:3), but by asserting His power over the nations that held them captive. The enemies of Israel could demand nothing of God, but unless His enslaved people saw His power they would not have the courage to claim their freedom.

The climax to this biblical concept of a high price to be paid for redemption came in the ministry of Jesus. Based on God's actions in the Old Testament (Isa. 43:3; Jer. 31:11), Jesus defined redemption in terms of a "ransom" sufficient to deliver the "many" from their bondage to sin (Mark 10:45). The costliness of that deliverance was dramatized in His death on the cross: "You know that you were *ransomed* from the futile ways inherited from your fathers, not with perishable things such as silver or gold, but with the *precious blood* of Christ" (1 Pet. 1:18-19, author's italics). In the way that He died, Jesus countered all of the hatred directed against Him with a love that was free to express unlimited forgiveness. He demonstrated obedience to a degree that equaled the rebellion of those who were determined to destroy Him. In other words, He met the full force of evil with a superior assertion of goodness. Even those who tried to coerce Him into conformity with their own bondage to legalism saw clearly that He could not be bought, that He did not have a price. In other words, they saw that *the price they were willing to pay to muzzle Him was not as great as the price He was willing to pay to liberate them!*

This "ransom" which Christ gave on behalf of the "many" was not some sentimental feeling in His heart but a concrete deed on a cross. In the ancient world, pagan gods were paid to free slaves from bondage, but this claim was a fiction for the slave had worked to save up his own ransom and so, in actuality, redeemed himself. An inscription at Delphi records, for example, how "Apollo the Pythian *bought* from Sosibius of Amphissa, *for freedom,* a female slave, whose name is Nicaea, by race a Roman, *with a price* of three minae of silver and a half-mina."[3] Paul alluded to such customs in saying that we who by nature are "*slaves* of sin" (Rom. 6:17) were "set . . . *free*" (Gal. 5:1) from bondage when we were "bought *with a price*" (1 Cor. 6:20; 7:23, author's italics). The decisive difference being that the Delphic god made no real payment whereas Christ paid with His life a fearful price which we were totally unable to pay.

Eventually this great truth, which at first was grounded in an event in history, came to be incorporated into a systematic doctrine of atonement. Over the centuries of its development, many theoretical questions have been discussed, one of the most controversial being that of to whom Jesus' "ransom" on the cross was paid. Some have supposed that it was paid to God in order to "satisfy" His wrath, but the New Testament clearly teaches that God was the initiator as well as the recipient of Calvary's sacrifice. Others have conjectured that Satan was paid off to secure the release of his hostages, but the New Testament teaches that he was decisively defeated at the cross and, hence, in no position to make such demands.

When a concert pianist thrills an audience with a virtuoso performance, we know that countless hours of study and practice were necessary to produce the end result. But to ask to whom such sacrificial effort was paid is futile, for it is the high price that anyone must pay who would play great music. Likewise, the soldier who lays down his life on the battlefield does not pay that supreme sacrifice to anyone. The real question is not *to* whom but *for* whom. The pianist pays the price for the sake of music, that beauty may be liberated from a black box with keys; the soldier pays the price for the sake of country, that its citizens may be delivered from the enemy; "Jesus Paid It All" for the sake of humanity that those in bondage to sin might be set free!

The Promise

When the plight of our human bondage is met by the price of Christ's precious blood, the result is the promise of spiritual freedom. To "ransom" is not merely to "pay a price," it is also thereby to release a victim from captivity. A typical New Testament expression of this is found in

Colossians 1:13-14: "He [the Father] has *delivered* us from the *dominion* of darkness and *transferred* us to the kingdom of his beloved Son, in whom we have *redemption*" (author's italics). Note that we are not set free from all sovereignties but are shifted from a despot who enslaves to the King who liberates. Our freedom is not inherent but acquired, not earned but conferred, not automatic but dependent upon the saving work of Christ.

The New Testament is rather specific about the before and after of redemption. It likes to list that we "were once slaves of sin" but "[now we are] set free from," especially: (1) sin (Rom. 6:17-18), that is, its passions and pleasures (Titus 3:3); (2) the law (Gal. 4:5), that is, the curse of being unable to meet its demands (Gal. 3:13); and (3) death (Rom. 7:24-25), that is, the "bondage to decay" (Rom. 8:21). The agents of oppression who have been overthrown are sometimes identified as "men" (1 Cor. 7:23), at other times as "powers" (Col. 2:15). Such references suggest that the scope of redemption is intended to be both inward and outward, both personal and social, both mental and physical. Some tyrannies are rooted in the passions, and thus are a matter of mood and mind-set, while others are rooted in what Paul called "principalities" and are thus a matter of collective forces, what we might call "power structures" hostile to human well-being. But whatever the threat, the gospel seeks to liberate us from every form of servitude that limits our God-given freedom.

Once this vision of freedom moves from the individual out to the larger society, it does not stop until it embraces the entire universe. In a breathtaking passage in Romans 8, the apostle Paul looked to a new age when the "creation itself will be set free from its bondage to decay and obtain the glorious liberty of the children of God" (v. 21). Here redemption is set in a cosmic context as the power that will finally overcome the sense of futility that infects a fallen creation (v. 20). But this ultimate goal is not wishful thinking; rather, it will happen when "the whole creation" comes to share in the emancipation which Christians have already begun to experience. The "children of God" constitute, as it were, a clearing in which is foreshadowed the "glorious liberty" made possible by the "first fruits of the Spirit" (v. 23; compare 2 Cor. 3:17).

As this spacious concept in Romans 8 makes clear, redemption has been inaugurated but is not yet consummated. It dawned with the victorious death of Christ, but its day is not yet complete (Eph. 4:30). We have begun to taste spiritual freedom, but we wait in hope for "the redemption of our bodies" (Rom. 8:23). Because we live in anticipation of a yet greater fulfillment, we dare not lapse back into slavery again (Gal. 2:4; 5:1; 1 Cor. 7:23). In the ancient world it was expressly forbidden, sometimes under the threat of heavy penalties, to enslave again any who had ever earned their freedom.[4] That prohibition was reinforced by declaring that freed slaves were now the property, and hence the protégés, of the god who had ransomed them from their former masters. In like manner Paul insisted that Christians were not free to revert to slavery because they were not their own (1 Cor. 6:19b); that is, they were the possession of the Christ who bought them, hence they were bound to Him for all time and eternity.

The distinguished anthropologist, Loren Eiseley, has given us an unforgettable illustration of the superiority of freedom to bondage. Eiseley's book *The Immense Journey* tells of the time when he captured a sparrow hawk while on an expedition to secure wildlife for a zoo. As he prepared to build a cage for his captive, Eiseley scanned the sky in vain for the mate who had escaped when the nest was raided. The author then described what happened as he took the young male out of the box in which he had been confined overnight:

> He lay limp in my grasp and I could feel his heart pound under the feathers but he only looked beyond me and up. I saw him look that last look away beyond me into a sky so full of light that I could not follow his gaze. . . . I suppose I must have had an idea then of what I was going to do, but I never let it come into consciousness. I just reached over and laid the hawk on the grass.
>
> He lay there a long minute without hope, unmoving, his eyes still fixed on that blue vault above him. It must have been that he was already so far away in heart that he never felt the release from my hand. He never even stood. He just lay with his breast against the grass.
>
> In the next second after that long minute he was gone. Like a flicker of light, he had vanished with my eyes full on him, but without actually seeing even a premonitory wing beat. He was gone straight into that towering emptiness of light and crystal that my eyes could scarcely bear to penetrate. For another long moment there was silence. I could not see him. The light was too intense. Then from far up somewhere a cry came ringing down.
>
> I was young then and had seen little of the world, but when I heard that cry my heart turned over. It was not the cry of the hawk I had captured; for, by shifting my position against the sun, I was now seeing further up. Straight out of the sun's eyes, where she must have been soaring restlessly

above us for untold hours, hurtled his mate. And from far up, ringing from peak to peak of the summits over us, came a cry of such unutterable and ecstatic joy that it sounds down across the years and tingles among the cups on my quiet breakfast table.

I saw them both now. He was rising fast to meet her. They met in a great soaring gyre that turned to a whirling circle and a dance of wings. Once more, just once, their two voices, joined in a harsh wild medley of question and response, struck and echoed against the pinnacles of the valley. Then they were gone forever somewhere into those upper regions beyond the eyes of men.[5]

As in the parables of Jesus, nature has again provided a glimpse of what it is like to be free. Christianity was never intended to be a cage confining the human spirit. Our hearts pound within us as we chafe under human restrictions and look beyond them to the firmament of eternity. Often we lie still for "a long minute without hope," not yet realizing that we have really been set free. But then, "from far up somewhere a cry comes ringing down." It is the gospel of God who hurtles straight out of the sun to call us to Himself. And, oh, when we soar with the wings of an eagle and rise to meet him "somewhere in those upper regions beyond the eyes of men," we discover the "unutterable and ecstatic joy" that comes from being redeemed!

Notes

1. Robert G. Lee, "Bought and Brought from Bondage by the Blessed Blood," *Pulpit Digest,* December 1955, pp. 17-18.

2. Eugene O'Neill, cited in *Cultural Information Service.*

3. Adolf Deissmann, *Light from the Ancient East,* rev. 3rd ed. (New York: Harper & Brothers, n.d.), p. 323.

4. Ibid., p. 325.

5. Loren Eiseley, *The Immense Journey* (New York: Random House, 1946), pp. 190-92.

Bibliography

Lochman, Jan M. *Reconciliation and Liberation: Challenging a One-Dimensional View of Salvation.* Philadelphia: Fortress Press, 1980. 159 pages.

Robinson, H. Wheeler. *Redemption and Revelation in the Actuality of History*. London: Nisbet & Co., 1942. Pages 195-312.

Sherrill, Lewis Joseph. *Guilt and Redemption*. Revised edition. Richmond: John Knox Press, 1957. 255 pages.

Whale, John S. *Victor and Victim: The Christian Doctrine of Redemption*. London: Cambridge University Press, 1960. 172 pages.

11
Reconciliation

Our best-known nursery rhymes endure because they describe the human condition in simple images that even a child can understand. Consider, for example, this picture of a brokenness that seems beyond any hope of repair:

> Humpty Dumpty sat on a wall,
> Humpty Dumpty had a great fall;
> All the king's horses
> And all the king's men
> Couldn't put Humpty Dumpty together again.

Ours is an age of fragmentation. Colonial empires break up into more Third World nations than we can name or locate on a map. Christian denominations continue to grow in number even in our stable country; a recent study catalogs 1,187 "primary denominations" in the United States.[1] The home seems just as unstable. Half the marriages now being made are doomed to end in divorce, reducing the average length of all American marriages to under ten years! Political parties are undergoing massive realignment as voter loyalties shift from one election to the next. Once stable business corporations are now involved in so many buy-outs, sell-offs, and mergers that even stockholders can hardly keep up with who owns what. Our whole culture is rent by cleavages: between eggheads and hard hats, between urban and rural, between sun belt and frost belt.

We need not belabor our brokenness; it is all about us for anyone to see. But if "all the king's horses And all the king's men" can't reassemble our shattered existence, then who can overcome that alienation, heal that estrangement, and rebuild that cohesiveness which we have lost at the center of life? The apostle Paul had no doubt that Jesus Christ could put broken lives back together again. To this restoration of unity he gave the name *reconciliation,* a term so distinctive that it had no religious usage in the Old Testament or in the Graeco-Roman world. By linking reconciliation to key concepts, such as justification, Paul made clear that he considered this achievement of wholeness to be a central component in the Christian experience of salvation.

Let us look at what the New Testament says about reconciliation in the four Pauline passages that discuss the oneness which Christ provides (Rom. 5:10-11; 2 Cor. 5:18-20; Eph. 2:14-16; Col. 1:18b-22a).

The Source of Reconciliation

The Subject Is God

Many people begin with an erroneous idea of reconciliation by supposing that, because God is good and we are bad, we are the ones who must do something to "make up" with God. Such efforts to placate God's anger against our sin might include professing one's faith, praying for acceptance, or offering some sacrifice. But not once in the New Testament does it say that God is reconciled by anything that we do. In fact, our passages do not even say that God does something to reconcile Himself to us. Rather, in every case God is said to reconcile us to Himself. The root idea in the Greek word for *reconciliation* is that of "change" or "transformation," and the Pauline usage makes clear that reconciliation is not a matter of our changing God's attitude toward us but of God changing our attitude toward Him.

Most people understand the various religions of the world as offering different ways to get right with God, whether through prescribed ritual or dogma or conduct. But New Testament Christianity insists that we are reconciled *to* God *by* God. The initiative lies entirely on the divine side. This is implied in all four of our primary passages but stressed especially in 2 Corinthians. The opening words set the tone: "*All this* is from *God* who . . . reconciled us *to himself*" (5:18). The same emphasis continues in the next verse but is sometimes muted by our punctuation of the phrase "God was in Christ." What verse 19 says is that, in the life, death, and resurrection of Christ, "*God was reconciling* the world to himself" (author's italics).

The Object Is Humanity

Unlike the usage in other religious literature contemporary with the New Testament, such as the Jewish Apocrypha, humanity is never the subject but is always the object of the verb "to reconcile." Mankind cannot *achieve* reconciliation with God but can only *receive* it from God. This is why Romans 5:11 says that our rejoicing is "in God" because through His sending of Christ "we have now *received* our reconciliation" (author's italics).

Why did New Testament writers take such pains to root the act of reconciliation entirely in God and never in human work? It is because of the dramatically different attitudes which the two parties bring to the problem of alienation. In the divine-human encounter, God comes as our lover, supremely shown through the giving of His only Son, Jesus Christ; whereas we come as God's "enemy" in a state of open rebellion. Note that it was "*while* we were *enemies*" that we were reconciled to God (Rom. 5:10), a contention which reinforced the earlier statement that "God shows his *love* for us in that *while we were yet sinners* Christ died for us" (v. 8, author's italics). The point is not that our sincere efforts at reconciliation are somehow flawed or inadequate. Rather, when God set about to bridge the gulf that separated Him from His creation, we did not have the slightest interest in assisting with such an effort because we "were estranged and hostile in mind, doing evil deeds" (Col. 1:21).

At first it may seem like an excessively harsh view of humanity to say that God offered an outstretched hand of love at the very moment when we were shaking a clenched fist of anger. But Paul's desire was not to discount the honest efforts of decent folk to find their way back to God. Instead, his intention in this blanket condemnation was to offer hope to everyone! If God would act to reconcile even His most belligerent foes, then we may be forever confident that He wants each of us to be reconciled as well. No opposition on our part is fierce enough to thwart His initiative. Paul was not mocking our religious aspirations by calling us God's "enemies." Rather, he was pleading with us never to give up on ourselves or any other person as being so bad as to be beyond the pale of reconciliation. The good news is: If "enemies" can be saved, *then anybody* can be saved!

The Scope of Reconciliation

The Potential Is the Cosmos

Paul's emphasis on "enemies" was really a way of universalizing the reach of reconciliation. The strategy was much like that in Romans 1:18 to 3:20 which Paul later summarized as: "God has consigned all men to disobedience, that he may have mercy upon all" (Rom. 11:32). This same point was made in positive fashion by Paul's affirmation that "God was reconciling *the world* to himself" (2 Cor. 5:19, author's italics). The Greek word for "world" is *kosmos* which suggests, as does our English derivative *cosmic,* that the entire created universe was included in the scope of God's action. In other words, God's provision was as comprehensive as humanity's plight. Because *everyone* is to some extent alienated from God by their "trespasses" (2 Cor. 5:19), God gives *everyone* a chance to become a part of His "new creation" (v. 17).

Just as Paul used both "enemies" and "trespasses" to show our universal need, so he used two other expressions, in addition to "cosmos," to show reconciliation's universal scope. First, in Ephesians 2:16 he spoke of how *"both"* Jews and Gentiles alike might be "reconciled to God in one body." In the ancient world, Jewish writers such as Paul viewed all humanity as being divided into those two groups, hence to say that "both" groups are included in God's reconciliation was a way of saying that everyone is included! Second, in Colossians 1:20 Paul said that God reconciled "to himself *all things,* whether on earth or in heaven" (author's italics). The phrase "all things" *(ta panta)* is an absolute expression which might literally be translated "the All" and understood here to express the limitless reach of God's reconciliation.

The Actual Is the Church

Precisely because God's reconciliation is cosmic in character, it can be promised to every person who will accept it. That is why all four of these passages include a call to decision. Romans 5:10 states that all of God's enemies were reconciled, but in verse 11 only those who "have *now received*" (author's italics) reconciliation rejoice in God. Second Corinthians 5:19 states that the world has been reconciled to God as an indicative fact, but verse 20 urges persons to "be reconciled to God" as an imperative necessity. Ephesians 2:16 pictures the reconciliation of both segments of society, Jews and Gentiles, but only those who are now together "in one body" have experienced the end of hostility between them. Colossians 1:20 announced the reconciliation of "all things" but then limits it to those who are becoming "holy and blameless and irreproachable" by continuing "in the faith, stable and steadfast" (vv. 22-23).

How are we to understand the relationship between reconciliation as it is achieved by God on a limitless scale and as it is received by human beings on a limited scale? On the one hand, the divine act is all-sufficient. There is nothing more that God needs to do. The ground of our confidence in God's reconciliation is complete. But, on the other hand, each individual must internalize the implications of God's work for his or her life in order for it to become effective. Only the community of faith can confess that it is now reconciled, for the church is the realm where God's reconciliation has already been realized in human affairs. But the church never views itself as a "favored few" who alone are reconciled because it knows that all of the other people in the world, however rebellious, can be reconciled if only they will accept God's gracious provision by faith.

The New Testament emphasis falls initially on the adequacy and finality of God's act, on the boundless reach of His grace, on His sovereign power to subdue all of the enmity of a hostile universe. But the emphasis then shifts to the need for a transformed community to bear witness to these truths and to beseech others to accept the same offer that is already changing their lives. The tension between God's *limitless* achievement and man's *limited* acceptance of it keeps the evangelistic imperative strong. We now turn to that ministry by looking more closely at the way in which God's reconciliation is mediated to others.

The Service of Reconciliation

The Ministry of Christ

All of our texts emphasize that Jesus Christ was the unique agent of God's reconciling activity. At times Paul said that reconciliation came *through* or *by* means of Christ (Rom. 5:10-11; 2 Cor. 5:18; Col. 1:20). At other times Paul varied the preposition and said that reconciliation was effected *in* the flesh or body of Christ (2 Cor. 5:19; Eph. 2:15; Col. 1:22). In both cases, the emphasis falls on the unique sacrifice of Christ at Calvary as the focus of God's reconciling activity. This sacrifice is referred to as Christ's death (Rom. 5:10), as His cross (Eph. 2:16), and as His blood (Col. 1:20), all three expressions being synonymous.

Unlike some medieval theories of the atonement, the New Testament does not emphasize that the crucifixion of Christ was a sacrificial offering intended to satisfy the wrath of God. Instead, it was viewed as an unforgettable expression both of the love of God for His bitterest enemies and of the hatred of man for his dearest friend. At the cross, Jesus identified so totally with the purpose of God that He became the perfect embodiment of God's seeking love that will endure any pain to reclaim a wayward child. At the same time, Jesus identified so totally with the plight of mankind that He became the perfect embodiment of that utter desolation which we all feel when the relationship with God is ruptured by sin. In one sense, reconciliation and alienation were fully joined in the death of Jesus, which is why we may bring the depths of our estrangement to His cross and there discover God's boundless acceptance.

The Ministry of Christians

The uniqueness and finality of Christ's death do not mean that God's reconciling activity is concentrated exclusively there. Instead, the cross is the fixed point from which Christ's followers participate in an ongoing process of reconciliation in His name. Paul called this "the ministry of reconciliation" which we have neither earned nor deserved but which God freely "gave" to us in the act by which He reconciled us to Himself (2 Cor. 5:18). That is but another way of saying that service is inherent in salvation. In this case, our role is that of an ambassador. An ambassador speaks not for himself but for the sovereign whom he represents. When we beseech others to "be reconciled to God," it is as if God Himself is "making his appeal through us" (2 Cor. 5:20).

Christians themselves do not reconcile others to God. Rather, Christians point others to Christ through whom God reconciles persons unto Himself. God alone can cancel trepasses (2 Cor. 5:19), but we can declare that message as His authorized representatives. At times one hears the church referred to as a "reconciling community," as if reconciliation were primarily a matter of achieving harmonious relationships between Christians. It is more correct to view the church, not as the agent of reconciliation, but as its mouthpiece. Paul was very careful to identify Christ as the exclusive agent who reconciles us "*to* God *in* one body *through* the cross" (Eph. 2:16, author's italics). The church, in other words, is where we *express* reconciliation but not where we *secure* it. Christians both individually and collectively are to point beyond themselves to Christ who alone is "our peace" (Eph. 2:14).

The Significance of Reconciliation

The Reality of Reconciliation

The central image suggested by the term *reconciliation* is that of *oneness*. Such unity may be created by joining together that which is separated, by mending that which is broken, or by removing barriers to harmony. Ephesians 2:14-16 emphasizes this theme by affirming that Christ made both Jew and Gentile "one" by breaking down "the dividing wall of hostility" between them (v. 14). But Christ did not leave Jew and Gentile to resolve their differences on their own once the barrier between them was abolished. Instead, He created *"in himself"* an entirely new humanity "in place of the two" that previously existed (v. 15). Notice how Paul piled up the uses of his key word "one" in describing this situation: "The *"one* new man" was reconciled to God "in *one* body" and given "access in *one* Spirit to the Father" (vv. 15,16,18, author's italics).

The characteristics of this profound new harmony are not hard to see. Three are singled out for emphasis: (1) The most prominent is *peace,* that cessation of hostilities which once made us enemies both of God and of other human groups (Eph. 2:14-17). (2) Another is *joy,* that lyric sense of spiritual ecstasy which replaces the mood of mutiny and rebellion (Rom. 5:11). (3) A final strand is that new sense of *access* to God which makes Him an ever-present Companion rather than a remote, mysterious stranger. The most striking thing about all three of these affirmations is that they are set forth in such dramatic contrast to the situation which they replaced. Reconciliation is, indeed, an incredible transformation: from hostility to peace, from bitterness to joy, from denial to access.

The Results of Reconciliation

The fruit of this fundamentally altered situation are described most comprehensively in Scripture by means of a series of contrasts running through Ephesians 2:11-22. The basic format of the passage is determined by an introductory formula: *Once* you were like that (v. 11) but *now* you are like this (v. 13). It is as if the two ages before and after Christ have been personalized so that each Christian can put a BC and an AD on his or her own calendar. Note the description of each era:

BC	AD
1. Separated from Christ (v. 12)	1. Fellow citizens with the saints (v. 19)
2. Alienated from Israel (v. 12)	2. Members of the household of God (v. 19)
3. Strangers to promise (v. 12)	3. No longer strangers (v. 19)

4. Having no hope (v. 12)   4. No longer sojourners (v. 19)
5. Without God (v. 12)   5. A dwelling place of God
(v. 22)

What all of these differences signify are two dramatically different ways to live. The alienated life is defined essentially as one of animosity, a running civil war with God. This leads to isolation and loneliness, separation from the sources of vitality and renewal. The reconciled life, by contrast, is one of acceptance, of belonging to God and to His family. The outsider becomes an insider, the alien becomes a citizen, the one who once felt "far off" now feels "near" (Eph. 2:13). Ultimately, therefore, the difference is one of identity. The alienated never quite know who they are because they belong only to themselves, whereas the reconciled discover who they are because of a new relationship with Christ and His people. To that new relationship we shall turn in the next chapter.

Note

1. J. Gordon Melton, *A Directory of Religious Bodies in the United States* (New York: Garland Publishing, 1977); *Encyclopedia of American Religions* (Wilmington, N.C.: McGrath Publishing, 1978).

Bibliography

Crabtree, Arthur Bamford. *The Restored Relationship: A Study in Justification and Reconciliation*. Valley Forge: Judson Press, 1963. 208 pages.

Denney, James. *The Christian Doctrine of Reconciliation*. New York: George H. Doran, 1918. 339 pages.

Harkness, Georgia Elma. *The Ministry of Reconciliation*. Nashville: Abingdon Press, 1971. 160 pages.

Hull, William E. *Beyond the Barriers*. Nashville: Broadman Press, 1981. 143 pages.

Martin, Ralph P. *Reconciliation: A Study of Paul's Theology*. Atlanta: John Knox Press, 1981. 262 pages.

Part IV
The Challenge

As we begin the fourth and final section of this study, it may prove helpful to remember the ground that we have covered thus far. Essentially, we have viewed salvation as an experience of divine change in human life so momentous that it may be called regeneration, adoption, and conversion (Part II). This transformation is made possible by an opening of life to God through repentance, faith, and confession (Part I). It results in a fundamentally new status, relationship, and identity with God as well as with others that may be described in terms of forgiveness, justification, redemption, and reconciliation (Part III).

The most curious thing about these three great stages in the pilgrimage of salvation is that so many people stop in their understanding when they reach this point. In one sense we could say that all three of these "movements" cluster around the *beginning* of the salvation symphony. On the day that one becomes Christian, it is correct to affirm that all ten of the realities surveyed in Parts I-III have become components of one's spiritual experience. To be sure, all of them have enduring results that will be deepened over many years of discipleship, but they are associated in most people's minds almost exclusively with the "front end" of the salvation process.

But does salvation have a "far end" that is equally important? The reason our neglect of this dimension is so curious is that, in the New Testament, *the center of gravity of the salvation experience lies in the future!* Despite all of the changes that we have now taken ten chapters to describe, the cry of the early Christians was, "Beloved, we are God's children *now;*" nevertheless, "it does *not yet* appear what we shall be" (1 John 3:2). Some of the texts cited in chapter 1 speak of salvation as a future expectation, such as "salvation is *nearer* to us now than when we first believed" (Rom. 13:11). Others include the passages on waiting, such as "Christ, . . . will appear a second time, not to deal with sin but *to save* those who are eagerly waiting for him" (Heb. 9:28). Then, of course, there are the verses on enduring, such as "he who endures to the *end* will be *saved*" (Matt. 10:22; 24:13, author's italics).

The issue is not just the importance of a future life in heaven. In fact, it would be a serious mistake to jump from front-end conversion to far-end consummation because such a move would overlook the crucial importance of discipleship as an integral part of the salvation experience. Close ties need to be maintained between evangelism and nurture, between planting and growing, between the starting power and the staying power that are both needed to live out the Christian life in its fullness. For this to happen, salvation must have a horizon as well as a memory, a hope as well as a faith, an ever-new frontier which keeps taut the tension between *now* and *not yet*.

This entire section is essentially a commentary on the imperative of Philippians 2:12-13: "Work out your own salvation with fear and trembling; for God is at work in you, both to will and to work for his good pleasure." Part III clarified four aspects of the divine "inworking" to serve as the foundation for our human "outworking." The challenge now before us may be put as follows: Since "God is at work in [us]" to forgive, justify, redeem, and reconcile, then how may we worthily respond by working out the implications of this salvation for as long as we shall live? The answer of Scripture is that we may do so by experiencing the fullness of life in Christ, the sanctifying power of the Holy Spirit, the assurance that our confidence is not in vain, the power to persevere in spite of temptation, and the certainty that "he who began a good work" in us will bring it to glorious completion "at the day of Jesus Christ" (Phil. 1:6).

12
Life

Visitors to the Vatican in Rome seek out the Sistine Chapel where they stare in wonder at the frescoes of Michelangelo Buonarroti stretched across its ceiling. In pride of place is the most famous panel in the series depicting *The Creation of Man*. To the left is the figure of Adam, said to be the most perfect representation of the human form ever painted. Adam's body languishes on its side, expectant but inert, waiting for the spark that will arouse it into action. The eye follows the form of the body to its focus in the finger of Adam, dangling passively at the end of an outstretched arm. To the right is the figure of God, so bristling with power that it seems to be moving across the ceiling. Here also the focus is on God's finger at the end of His outstretched arm, but with what a difference! The divine finger is taut with strength as it reaches forth to touch the limp finger of Adam.[1]

The artist captured the divine-human encounter at that point of contact where life is transferred from Creator to creature. In so doing, Michelangelo depicted in dramatic form the answer of Scripture to the central question of our existence. More than anything else we are looking for life, not just physical life without which our bodies would perish, but also spiritual life without which our souls would languish, as did Adam's even within his magnificent physique. That is why we abhor a "dead" church or a "lifeless" party or an "empty" marriage. Always we need life, as urgently as we need air to breathe, because life is synonymous with energy, vitality, and strength. To every person searching for a dynamic existence, the Bible declares what Michelangelo painted: God has the touch that can quicken the very core of our being and make us come alive!

The simple four-lettered word *life* is so central and comprehensive a concept that it is used in Scripture as a synonym for salvation. The saying of Jesus, "I came that they may have *life,* and have it abundantly" (John

10:10), is equivalent to saying, "I came that they may have *salvation, and have it abundantly.*" In the Gospel of John, the usage of *life* as salvation is elaborated in the teaching that Jesus is "the *life*" (14:6), hence the words that He spoke offer "spirit and *life*" (6:63) which, if we accept them, give to us *life* that is "eternal" (3:15-16,36). Elsewhere in the New Testament, Paul paralleled these statements by claiming that Christ is "our *life*" (Col. 3:4), that His gospel which we are to hold fast is "the word of *life*" (Phil. 2:16), and that we are raised through baptism to "walk in newness of *life*" (Rom. 6:4, author's italics). No wonder J. B. Lightfoot commented that Christianity in "its substance is neither a dogmatic system nor an ethical code, but a Person and a Life."[2]

In coming to this consideration of salvation as life, we shift in subtle ways from a negative to a positive perspective. Most of the dimensions of salvation treated in earlier chapters were seen against the dark backdrop of human sin; that is, they described salvation in terms of the plight from which the believer was being rescued. But the present chapter, and those to follow, deal with dimensions of salvation flowing from the changes described earlier and so assume the brighter backdrop of the conversion process already underway. C. A. Anderson Scott pointed up this contrast very nicely:

> We have examined the factors of salvation in its negative aspect; what is common to all three factors of Salvation in that aspect, Redemption, Justification, Reconciliation, is that each of them depends on something accomplished by the *death* of Christ. What is common to the factors of Salvation in its positive aspect is that they are intimately connected with His *life,* the life of one who "has been crucified," but is "alive for evermore." "*Much more* shall we be *saved* by his *life*."[3]

Life in God

From the outset, the Bible rejects a naturalistic understanding of life such as found in modern vitalism. Life is not viewed in Scripture as immanent in the entire universe, inherent in all living things simply as a part of their nature. Rather, all life is seen to root uniquely and exclusively in God who bestows it as the climactic act of divine creation (Gen. 2:7). One of the most significant attributes of God in the Old Testament is that He is the "living God" (Deut. 5:26; Josh. 3:10; 1 Sam. 17:26) or "the God who lives" (see Num. 14:28; Deut. 32:40; Ruth 3:13). If life refers to the dynamic force at the heart of all existence, then God *is* life, almost by definition, since He is the ultimate source of the vital energies pulsating through the universe. The most characteristic thing that can be said about the God of the Bible, in contrast to idols, is that He is *alive!* He thinks and feels; He takes the initiative and gets involved; He intervenes to act at the most surprising times (compare 1 Kings 18:27-29 with vv. 36-39).

Because God is, in Himself, the God of *life,* He is also, for those who relate to Him, the God of the *living.* Human nature is possessed of no innate immortality but survives only as it is infused with life as a gift of God. Conversely, death is not a natural phenomenon in the Bible, that is, it is not self-evident or inevitable, but occurs when God withdraws His life (Job 34:14-15; Ps. 104:29). The Sadducees, who did not believe in eternal life, once tried to trap Jesus into agreeing with their position by challenging Him to resolve the dilemma which heaven would present to a woman who had been married successively to seven brothers (Mark 12:18-23). In reply, Jesus rebuked them for a superficial understanding of their favorite Scripture passage on Moses at the burning bush, in which God said, "*I am* the God of Abraham, and the God of Isaac, and the God of Jacob," all of these being patriarchs long dead in the time of Moses. Concluded Jesus: Since "He is not God of the dead, but of the *living,*" the Sadducees were quite wrong in failing to realize that the power of God was sufficient not only to keep people alive long after their physical demise but also to resolve whatever problems they brought with them to heaven from their earthly existence (vv. 24-27, author's italics).

What this brilliant piece of biblical interpretation by Jesus teaches us is that when "the God of the living" becomes the God *of* a particular person—whether it be Abraham and Moses or you and me—then His divine life, which is as absolute and eternal as God Himself, infuses the life of that person and becomes its ultimate bulwark against destruction. A *living* relationship with God is just that, a linkage which permits persons to share the life of God in their own lives. This possibility is foreshadowed on the very first pages of the Bible where the creation of man is depicted as God breathing His own "breath of life" into the nostrils of man so that he "became a living being" (Gen. 2:7).

Supreme proof of the truth that we live only in God's life was provided in the earthly ministry of Jesus. Has anyone ever been more alive? He labored from dawn to dusk (see Mark 1:32-39) with an almost inexhaustible energy. Jesus' preaching possessed a commanding authority before which even the unclean spirits fell silent (see vv. 21-27). His miracles mediated a power great enough to snatch people back from the brink of death (see Mark 5:23,35,41-42). So strong was His presence that His disciples felt helpless in His absence (see Mark 4:37-38; 6:47-51; 9:17-18). He faced apparent disaster in Jerusalem with an unshakable confidence is eventual victory (John 16:33; 19:30). After brutal crucifixion, death, and burial, within three days He was back again, more alive than ever! What was eternally true of the preexistent Christ was historically true of the incarnate Christ: *"In him was life"* (John 1:4, author's italics).

We are not left to wonder about the source of Jesus' remarkable vitality. In the great intercessory prayer of John 17, Jesus summed up the significance of His entire ministry and explained how He had fulfilled His mission: "Thou, Father, art *in me* and I *in thee*" (v. 21). The ultimate clue to the uniqueness of Jesus is that His life was filled with the life of God! No sooner did Jesus disclose this mystery at the depths of His own being than He went on to make clear that the overriding purpose of His ministry was to extend that same relationship to His disciples: "that they *also* may be *in us*" (v. 21), "I *in them* and thou *in me*" (v. 23, author's italics). In other words, God was *in* Christ and Christ was *in* God so intimately that Jesus literally lived out the life of God on earth. But as the Mediator of divine life to others, Jesus prayed to be *in* His disciples and His disciples *in* Him so intimately that they would live out His life in their own.

In order to make this possible, Jesus promised to return to the disciples after death in the presence of the Holy Spirit. Note in the very first of five passages on the Paraclete in the farewell discourse of John 14—16 that the reason for returning in this fashion was so that Jesus' followers might "know," that is, experience for themselves, "that I am *in* my Father, and you *in* me, and I *in* you" (John 14:20, author's italics). This clearly emphasizes that the only place one can get life is from another life. It comes not from books or institutions but from people. Life is contagious, hence it is mediated in relationship, in mutuality, in reciprocity. To summarize: In order to live, we must somehow be given God's life, since His is the only life that endures. To be given God's life, we must enter into a personal relationship with Him; merely to hold beliefs about Him is not enough. Only one person has perfectly achieved that divine-human communion with God, and that was Jesus Christ, hence we must let Him relate to us so profoundly that we will thereby share His unique relationship with God.

Life in Christ

All of us know to some extent the galvanizing effect of charismatic leaders on their followers. Think of how Oliver Cromwell stamped his personality on Puritan England, how Adolf Hitler mesmerized a generation of disenchanted Germans, or how John F. Kennedy inspired the hope of a new Camelot in the United States. But their influence collapsed almost as soon as they died. Jesus' disciples dimly realized how devastated they would be by His premature departure (John 13:36; 14:11). Leadership requires *life*, thus if Jesus died a horrible death by crucifixion, would that leave them bereft of the incredible power which they had experienced for as long as He was with them?

In response, Jesus reassured them that they would not be left "orphaned" by an absentee Lord (John 14:18). Instead, because He was "*in*" the Father and the Father *in*" Him (v. 11), both He and His Father would come back to make their home with these frightened followers (v. 23). Furthermore, they would do so in the Spirit of the risen Christ, which meant that the fullness of the divine family would dwell in their midst. This promise was fulfilled immediately after the resurrection when Jesus appeared to His disciples triumphant over death (John 20:19-20). On the basis of that victory He did two things. First, He "sent" them on mission "as the Father" had sent Him (v. 21). Second, He empowered them for that mission by *breathing* on them and saying, "Receive the Holy Spirit" (John 20:22). Just as God's breathing His breath on human dust in creation had conveyed physical life (Gen. 2:7), so Jesus' breathing His risen power into the disciples conveyed spiritual life, new creation.

Sceptics may view this story with suspicion because the one thing that dead people lack is the "breath of life"! But the plain truth is that the Christian movement would have collapsed in the aftermath of the cross had it not received a fresh infusion of life following that awful tragedy. The fact that the faith not only survived but also flourished, and has done so for two thousand years, is proof positive that death at its very worst could not snuff out the divine life that energized the ministry of Jesus. Instead, it liberated His divine life for even more powerful expression. What the enemies of Jesus quickly discovered was that once that life had broken out of its tomb it could no longer be lashed with a whip, gigged with a spear, or crucified on a cross. In other words, with the resurrection of Jesus, the world discovered life in a new dimension: life not confined by time or place, life not threatened by death or hell, life that is "alive for evermore" (Rev. 1:18)!

A vivid example of that new life in action may be seen in the experience of Saul of Tarsus. Wrapped in the impregnable defenses of religious fanaticism, Saul set forth for Damascus in a futile effort to stamp out the life of the infant Christian movement there (Gal. 1:13-14), only to be encountered and overwhelmed by the ultimate source of its life in the exalted Lord of heaven (Acts 9:1-5). In essence, the conversion that transformed Saul of Tarsus into Paul the apostle was a conversion to *life*. As Anderson Scott put it, "Life with all the riches of its content, Life in God and to God . . . moved forward and enveloped him as an atmosphere, penetrated him as the fabric of a new personality."[4] On the Damascus road, Paul did not decide to adopt a new religion or morality; rather, he was given a new life. Henceforth, Paul's existence was characterized by an intensity and an impetus which it had never known before.

To this qualitatively new experience, Paul gave fresh expression, identifying it by the formula "in Christ," which was theological shorthand for the life that he now had in relationship to the Lord. For example, he was content to describe himself simply as "a man in Christ" (2 Cor. 12:2) and to let that self-designation stand for the "sharing" (see Phil. 3:10), the "fellowship" (1 Cor. 1:9), the "participation" (1 Cor. 10:16) which the believer enjoys in communion *(koinōnia)* with the divine. Paul's well-known versatility allowed him to speak either of the believer being "in Christ" (see Phil. 1:1) or of Christ being "in" the believer (see Rom. 8:10; Col. 1:27). Again, he could vary the preposition and speak of the believer experiencing something "with" Christ (see Rom. 6:8; 8:17). But in all these usages he was pointing to a mutual indwelling analogous to that by which God was *in* Christ and Christ was *in* God, both separate and yet one. Nor was this life "in Christ" viewed by Paul as a momentary spiritual "high" but as the permanent condition of all Christians from the time when they first believe.

Clearly Paul was claiming that Christ was not just an example but an experience, not just a pattern but a presence, not just a concept but a companion. All of us know the difference between being *out*side or *be*side or *in*side another person. The last of these means to see life from another's perspective: to think with his thoughts, to feel with his emotions, to act with his intentions. In psychology this is called "identification," in friendship it is called "empathy," in marriage it is called "union." Perhaps the best word to express the overarching reality is *inti-*

macy. Paul was not thinking of an absorptionistic mysticism by which the personalities of believers are swallowed up in Christ. Rather, he was describing a relationship made possible by the Holy Spirit through the preaching of the word according to which believers enter so deeply into the experience of Christ that they may say, as did he: "I have been crucified *with* Christ; it is no longer I who live, but Christ who lives *in* me; and the life I now live in the flesh I live by faith *in* the Son of God, who loved me and gave himself *for* me" (Gal. 2:20, author's italics).

The 164 uses of the "in Christ" formula in the writing of Paul may be divided into two main types. First, there is a "local" usage which identifies Christ as the sphere in which salvation is to be found. In this sense, Christ is the climate in which we live, the atmosphere we breathe, the place where we take our stand. Second, there is an "instrumental" usage which identifies Christ as the means by which that salvation is to be found. In this sense, Christ is the agent through whom the blessings of God are mediated to us. Both uses are closely interrelated, the local sense being more basic. The primary force of the preposition *in* emphasizes the *closeness* of the personal relationship which Christians sustain to Christ. There is no way to describe greater intimacy than to say that two persons are "in" each other!

Life in the Body

The description of salvation as life "in Christ" raises a problem we must now seek to solve. Usually we think of intimacy in terms of only two persons, such as husband and wife or bosom friends. Much talk about mysticism sounds very isolating, as if the soul is trying to escape earth to be "alone" with God. So the question obviously is whether the "in Christ" concept is too individualistic. If a third party is thought of as an intrusion into an uncluttered relationship which is possible between two persons, then how can the "in Christ" relationship be opened up to multitudes of believers without destroying its intimacy? What is so special about being "in Christ," some might ask, if millions of other persons enjoy the same privilege?

Paul was keenly aware that Christian existence as he understood it might be interpreted in terms of passionate subjectivity and that such subjectivity is only a step removed from an individualism that could dissolve the earthly bond between disciples. So Paul deliberately developed a basic metaphor with which to explain the social dimensions of life "in Christ," that of the *body*. By means of an extended commentary in

1 Corinthians 12:12-27, Paul explained why he chose that image: First, each of us has a body which we can never discard, hence the analogy is rooted in universal human experience. Second, clearly the body has "many members" (see v. 14) which are very diverse. Third, at the same time, all of these organs are indispensable, even those "unpresentable parts" (v. 23) which are never seen. Therefore, all of these varied components are to dwell together in harmony, constituting an organic whole which may be called "*one* body." We often speak of this arrangement as an example of *unity-in-diversity,* which is certainly true, but we might also describe it as *intimacy-in-multiplicity* because each member is a completely integral part of the body even thought there are many other parts with which it must coexist.

Applying these parallels to the Christian situation, Paul argued as follows: (1) Christ has a body, since in biblical thought a living personality is never "disembodied." (2) Christ's spiritual body is made up of those who are "*in* Christ" in the same way that arms and legs are attached to, and therefore inseparable from, a physical body. (3) Human diversity exists among the many who constitute the body of Christ just as biological diversity exists among the organs of a physical body. All of this variety is to be honored as essential to the functioning of the entire body. (4) When that is done, when there is genuine "care for one another" (v. 25), then we can say that the body of Christ is truly *one.* When that happens, the intimacy which we know "in Christ" is experienced, not as intimacy-in-*solitary,* but as intimacy-in-*solidarity.*

There are many profound implications to describing life "in Christ" as life in "the body" of Christ. For one thing, it gives an objective dimension to an otherwise subjective experience. "Life," as such, is so general and intangible as to be abstract, but life in a particular body is very specific and concrete. Inward communion with the cosmic Christ must be balanced by outward community with an earthly congregation. But, for another thing, this means that the intimacy that we enjoy with Christ because of *our* faith is extended to intimacy with others who share the same faith. There is no way to be drawn close to Christ without thereby being drawn close to every person who is "in Christ." That is why our personal fellowship *(koinōnia)* with Christ enlarges to become a "fellowship" which embraces the entire church (Acts 2:42). Those linked to Christ have more in common with each other, despite the differences that might otherwise divide them, than they do with those who seem most outwardly similar to them.

Christ enlivens all who are members of His body. When we were "in Adam" (1 Cor. 15:22; compare Rom. 5:12-21), caught up in solidarity with the sinful legacy of our human ancestry, we belonged to a "body of death" (Rom. 7:24). But now that we are "in Christ," we belong to a body that is alive in His Spirit (8:2-6). This is the only reason Paul could speak of "*all* the saints *in* Christ Jesus" (Phil. 1:1). Methodists today do not speak of being "*in* John Wesley," for Wesley is only a blessed memory, not a risen, living presence. The secret of Christian vitality for two thousand years roots in one thing only, in "Christ *who is our life*" (Col. 3:4, author's italics).

I believe that many readers of this book can verify that truth in their personal experience. All of us know something about the aging process by which anything alive, as it grows old, becomes listless and weary from diminished energy. Almost imperceptibly we begin to slow down as vitality slips away. Our step is a little slower, our hearing a little duller, our eyesight a little dimmer, our hair a little thinner. It is what we might call the "graying" of the flesh. But what about the Christ who may have come into your heart many years, even decades, ago? Is He any less vital, less dynamic, less powerful than in the hour when you first believed? The testimony of most Christians is that "every day with Jesus" is sweeter and richer and deeper "than the day before." Why should this be? Why should Christ not grow old as you grow old? Why, amid the graying of your flesh, should you experience the "greening" of your spirit? Why, in other words, do Christians come to the end of their earthly days with the certainly that life for them has just begun?

There is only one explanation for this phenomenon: The life of Christ within us is as deathless as the life of God Himself. The only adequate word for such life is *eternal*. And when we have eternal life, here and now, deep in the very core of our being, we know that we are truly being saved, both in this world and in the world to come.

Notes

1. For a likeness of the panel described, with an interpretation, see Cynthia Pearl Maus, *The Old Testament and the Fine Arts* (New York: Harper & Row, 1954), pp. 14-16.

2. J. B. Lightfoot, *Saint Paul's Epistle to the Philippians* (London: Macmillan, 1913), p. ix.

3. Charles A. Anderson Scott, *Christianity According to St. Paul* (Cambridge: University Press, 1961), p. 141. Italics added. The Scripture quotation is from Romans 5:10.

4. Ibid., p. 137.

Bibliography

Best, Ernest. *One Body in Christ*. London: S.P.C.K., 1955. 250 pages.

Bloesch, Donald G. *The Christian Life and Salvation*. Grand Rapids: Wm. B. Eerdmans, 1967. 164 pages.

Smedes, Lewis B. *All Things Made New: A Theology of Man's Union with Christ*. Grand Rapids: Wm. B. Eerdmans, 1970. 272 pages.

Stewart, James S. *A Man in Christ: Vital Elements of St. Paul's Religion*. New York: Harper and Brothers, n.d. 332 pages.

13

Sanctification

Have you ever reflected on the fact that, no matter how large a building may be, it is usually entered through a small door? For example, all of the cultural riches crammed into a vast museum are offered to us only if we are willing to go through an entry scarcely bigger than the human body. Words are like doors to the reality which they describe. If the name which we give to some doctrine is daunting, we may never step across the threshold and go beyond the label to the truth for which it stands.

Sanctification is such a word. Its very sound is so heavy that we decide not to ask what it means. Nor is it a term on the tip of our tongues in daily conversation. I doubt if anyone has ever come up to you, even at church, and asked, "Are you feeling sanctified today?" Actually, the biblical vocabulary which we translate into English as *sanctity* and related terms also stands behind the word groupings related to *saint,* to *holy* or *holiness,* and to *hallowed*—language reserved primarily for use by preachers in Sunday sermons. It is difficult for a reality to enter significantly into our understanding or experience if we almost never use the terminology to describe it.

But the problem is greater than our neglect of a strange vocabulary. In my first pastorate, a deep South rural congregation, a religious sect in the community majored on sanctification in its approach to the Christian faith. Women members were called "Black Stockings" because they literally wore thick woolen stockings year round, even in the hottest summer, believing that it was indecent to expose any part of their legs through sheer hose. Whether intended or not, this "holiness" group fostered the popular impression that sanctification referred to such things as using no makeup and wearing dresses reaching below the ankle. Some of you may have had experiences that cause you to associate the subject of this chapter with various types of religious extremism or bizarre behavior.

It would be a pity, however, if we let any negative meanings clustering around such words as *sanctified/holy/saint* make us reluctant to explore the rich meanings of the reality to which they point. After all, the concept of consecration, which these several terms seek to describe, is a dominant emphasis throughout the Bible. A check of the relevant vocabulary in a concordance will show this. Moreover, a neglect of this massive scriptural teaching can only lead to a distorted doctrine of salvation. To avoid that danger, let us put aside all inherited stereotypes of what sanctification may mean and make a fresh effort to recover that balanced perspective which we find in the Word of God.

Despite the complexity of our English translations, the basic meaning of the biblical terminology is relatively simple. The root idea is that of *separateness,* of being set apart in the sense of being different and distant, above and beyond. The primary application of the concept is to the uniqueness of God, to God's being "high and lifted up" (Isa. 6:1). Carlyle Marney used to speak of this radical otherness by saying that God's "holiness" is His "onliness," that is, His being the One whose thoughts are not our thoughts and whose ways are not our ways (Isa. 55:8). This does not mean, however, that the holiness of God refers only to His transcendence in the sense of a remote detachment from the human scene. In Hosea 11, God's heart "recoils" (v. 8) as He considered how His people "are bent on turning away from me" (v. 7). But because His "compassion grows warm and tender" (v. 8), God decided, "I will *not* execute my fierce anger" (v. 9). The point is that God can make such a decision to be different "for I am God and not man, the *Holy One* in your midst" (v. 9, author's italics).

Now we see that God's holiness roots in His distinctiveness as God and in His self-determination to honor that distinctiveness regardless of what pressures are placed on Him to act otherwise. In this sense, God's sanctity is His sovereignty, that is, His unshakable insistence on *being God!* It is not accidental that the first petition of the Lord's Prayer is "Hallowed [sanctified or made holy] be thy name" (Matt. 6:9). Since "name" stands for one's identity, what Jesus was teaching us is that it is imperative for God to be known *as He really is* and not as we might like for Him to be known. To paraphrase: "God, be Yourself, and let us accept You for all that You really are!"

This insight prepares us to understand the secondary sense in which the Bible can relate sanctification to the experience of salvation. Since God is holy in that He is utterly sovereign and indescribably sublime, then how may that awesome reality be attributed to anything earthly? The answer is that such a transference is possible only when the human is touched by the divine. The transcendent God must invade our world and infuse that which is profane with that which is holy. Thus sanctification in the human sense involves putting our lives and our possessions at God's disposal, allowing them to be set aside for use in God's service. In a very real sense, then, sanctification may be described as the *experience of godliness,* the sharing of a holiness that is not ours but may be received from God. As such, it is a status to be conferred, a task to be undertaken, and a goal to be reached, all in fulfillment of the imperative, "Be holy, for I [the Lord your God] am holy" (Lev. 11:44).

The Spheres of Sanctification

Impersonal Spheres

In Scripture, sacredness is attached to anything set aside for use by the holy God. Even impersonal realities were considered sanctified if they had been dedicated to a divine purpose. We can trace a natural progression through the Bible of the way *holy* is used—from the impersonal to the personal arena. But the fact that nothing in all creation is off limits to God's sanctity shows that He intends eventually to infuse the whole of human existence with His holiness. Even the most commonplace aspects of life are candidates for sanctification.

Times.—The calendar itself could be consecrated to God. For example, the seventh day of each week was a Sabbath which was to be remembered to "keep it *holy*" (Ex. 10:8, author's italics). By that same pattern, every seventh year was to be a sabbatical year which bore to the six previous years the same relationship that the sabbath day bore to the other six days of the week (Ex. 23:10-13). Then after seven cycles of seven years each, the fiftieth year was called a year of Jubilee, which was "to be holy" to all the people (Lev. 25:8-12). Many other times on the Jewish calendar, such as the great annual festivals of Passover, Pentecost, and Tabernacles, were set aside as belonging to God.

Places.—Just as God could lay claim to time itself and invest particular periods with sanctity, so He could also assert lordship over space by marking off certain places as sacred. Think how naturally the Bible has taught us to refer to Palestine as the "*holy* land," with Jerusalem as its "*holy* city" (Isa. 52:1), Zion as its "*holy* mountain" (Isa. 27:13), and the Temple as its "*holy*" place (Ps. 65:4, author's italics). Wherever God appeared, even on the back side of the desert, that place was "holy ground" (Ex. 3:5). Behind numerous such references lay the conviction that God is not shut out of His world but that He can claim "turf" wherever He pleases, which thereby becomes sanctified with His presence.

Things.—Once God enveloped a particular place during a particular period, everything in that time-space continuum was touched with His holiness. The best example, of course, was the tabernacle in the wilderness and, later, the Temple in Jerusalem. The vestments worn by the priests were "holy garments" (Ex. 28:2-4), the meat and bread used in sacrifice were a "holy" offering (Ex. 29:31-34), even the vessels used in the worship service were so holy (1 Kings 8:4) that to approach them unworthily was to risk death (Num. 18:3). So holy was the ark of the covenant, the most sacred symbol of all, that to look inside it, or accidentally to touch it, could lead to fearful judgment (1 Sam. 6:19 to 7:1; 2 Sam. 6:6-7).

Personal Spheres

Even a primitive religion of animism believes that the "numen" or vital force of its deity can inhabit objects, such as rocks and trees, making them holy in the sense of being taboo. But the Bible moved far beyond such superstition by a long process of personalizing, internalizing, and individualizing its doctrine of holiness. We can trace this development in three stages through Scripture.

A holy people.—The writer of the Book of Deuteronomy was especially fond of referring to Israel as "a people holy to the Lord your God" (7:6; 14:2,21; 26:19; see 28:9) which meant "a people for his own possession" (7:6; 14:2; 26:18). Once the people established their political identity, they were to be a "holy nation" (Ex. 19:6). At first the concept reflected the powerful sense in which Israel felt itself to be uniquely chosen by God (Deut. 7:7), but in time the prophets gave to the concept an increasingly ethical emphasis.

A holy priesthood.—Within the nation, however, a special vocation of holiness was assigned to an increasingly select group of priests. At first it was to the entire tribe of Levi from among the twelve tribes of Israel (Deut. 10:8), then to the sons of Aaron from among that one tribe (Ex. 28:1,40-43), finally to the descendents of Zadok from among the Aaronic lineage. One reason for the narrowing process was that the people as a whole could not maintain the sanctity necessary for the service of God. Often the priests themselves lacked the purity needed to represent the entire nation before God. Therefore the hope of finding someone worthy to offer true sacrifice focused increasingly on a remnant of just a few, or even one, such as the Servant of the Lord (Isa. 53:10).

A holy person.—Jesus fulfilled the agelong quest of the Old Testament for a person so completely possessed by God and set apart for God's service as to be "the *Holy One* of God" (Mark 1:24, author's italics). All of the scriptural strands were gathered up in Jesus' earthly ministry. God so chose Him and sent Him and filled Him that Jesus perfectly embodied godliness in a human life. In a phrase, He was *sanctification incarnate!* Salvation in Christ is salvation unto a holiness that permeates the life of every believer (1 Thess. 4:7). To live "in Christ" is "to live . . . *godly* lives in this world" because Jesus Christ "gave himself for us . . . to *purify* for himself a *people of his own*" (Titus 2:12,14).

The Sources of Sanctification

By describing certain times and places and things and persons as holy or sanctified, the Bible is telling us *when* and *where* we may best find God. But once it has defined this sacred structure built into human existence, Scripture then tells us *how* the holiness which is to be found there may be mediated to us today. There are three primary sources of sanctification—upward, inward, and outward—which is but a way of pointing to three routes or channels by which godliness may flow into our lives as a crucial aspect of the Christian experience of salvation.

The Upward Source: Worship

The main reason the Old Testament set apart certain times and places as holy was so that the people might gather to worship God. The willingness of God to create a hallowed framework in which worship might happen was in itself proof that He would come to envelop the waiting people with His presence if only they would call upon Him to do so. Central to this experience in the New Testament was the ministry of the Word, understood primarily as the word which Jesus brought revealing God because He *was* the Word of God (John 1:1-18). In the "high priestly prayer" of John 17, Jesus declared that He had given to the disciples God's word (v. 14), then prayed to the Father, "*Sanctify* them in the truth: thy *word* is truth" (v. 17, author's italics). All of which is a way of saying that when the "living and active" word of God (Heb. 4:12) enters our lives and lodges there, it mediates nothing less than the God of whom it speaks, the God who makes us holy!

The Inward Source: Holy Spirit

God comes to us from above through worship, and He also comes to us from within through "the Spirit of holiness" by which Christ was raised from the dead (Rom. 1:4). We have heard a lot in recent years about *synergism,* a word which means "working together." The concept refers to the creative possibilities achieved by working with others rather than working alone. This term has been used for most of Christian history to describe the way in which the human and the divine cooperate in the creative transformation called salvation. In a very real sense, by bidding us to "walk by the Spirit" (Gal. 5:16), Paul was suggesting that the Christian life is a process of synergism with the indwelling Spirit of God. And since that Spirit is most characteristically called the *"Holy* Spirit," we cannot help but become holy as our lives are filled with the Spirit's presence. Several strands of our discussion are tied together in 2 Thessalonians 2:13, "God *chose* you . . . to be saved, through *sanctification* by the *Spirit* and belief in the *truth*" (author's italics).

The Outward Source: Fellowship

In modern usage, the term *saint* usually refers to a person of exceptional spiritual attainment; in the New Testament, it is almost always used in the plural to refer to all Christians. Paul typically began letters by addressing the members of a church as "saints." In 1 Corinthians Paul referred to the readers as "those *sanctified* in Christ Jesus, called to be *saints*" (1:2, author's italics), even though most of the letter dealt with lamentable shortcomings of which they were guilty! The holiness of the Corinthians consisted not in their personal piety but in the richness of the spiritual gifts which they received from God by virtue of their common fellowship with the Son, Jesus Christ (vv. 4-9). A church is a place where individual believers "pool" their spiritual resources for the good of one another. That rich word *fellowship (koinōnia)* means that each is to share his or her experience of God with others. By this means, the holiness of the whole body reinforces and undergirds the consecration of each member, however humble.

The Stages of Sanctification

The Bible makes clear that sanctification, like the salvation of which it is a part, takes place over a lifetime. There are no rigid steps prescribed in Scripture, but we can detect three stages or dimensions of sanctification which are characteristic of Christian experience. These categories follow very closely the temporal framework of past, present, and future in which our whole study of salvation has been set.

Sanctification as Gift

When Paul said that "God made" Christ Jesus "our . . . sanctification" (1 Cor. 1:30), he meant that the possibility of becoming holy was established as a divine gift entirely apart from our doing or deserving. Ultimately, because the Son of God was the perfect embodiment of holiness, every believer may be said to be "sanctified in Christ Jesus." An acquired holiness is planted at the core of our being before we do anything to make ourselves holy. In 1 Corinthians, Paul compiled a list of despicable sinners (6:9-10), only to add, "And such were some of you" (v. 11). Immediately, however, he contrasted this terrible indictment, "But you . . . *were sanctified* . . . in the name of the Lord Jesus Christ and in the Spirit of our God" (v. 11, author's italics). The passive voice denotes a sanctification *received* rather than *achieved,* while the past tense implies that such became an accomplished fact at the outset of the Christian life. Because this new status was conferred rather than earned, it may be said to refer to the new standing of a Christian in the sight of God and thus termed "positional sanctification."

Sanctification as Growth

If the first word of the gospel regarding sanctification is stated in the indicative mood, "You are already sanctified!" then the second word is in the imperative mood, "Strive . . . for the holiness without which no one will see the Lord" (Heb. 12:14). This relationship of imperative to indicative reproduces the famous Old Testament formula, "*Be* holy, for I *am* holy" (Lev. 11:44-45). Let what began at a point enlarge into a process. Let the gift of positional sanctification become foundational for growth in what we may call progressive sanctification. Let the potentiality latent in having the holy life of Christ living within our hearts become an actuality as true godliness spreads to all parts of our lives. None of this means, however, that we are to chase after sanctity as an elusive prize. Because Christ has sanctified us by His life, all of our subsequent efforts represent progress *in* a sanctification already assured rather than progress *toward* a sanctification not yet acquired.

Sanctification as Goal

Even though our strivings for holiness are to be in earnest, they are not to be forever. The eventual end of all our efforts was defined by Jesus in terms of a perfection like that of our heavenly Father (Matt. 5:48). Here we have, not the formal, but the material counterpart of Sinai's "Be holy, as I am holy." What sanctification makes clear is that *God's ultimate goal is to make us like Himself.* Since we are, in fact, made in the image of God (Gen. 1:26-27), godliness should be our highest destiny and the supreme purpose of our salvation. Thus to the previously discussed positional sanctification and progressive sanication, we must dare to add a third and final stage called perfective sanctification.

Many sincere Christians are afraid to press sanctification this far because of the way in which some holiness groups have used the teachings of Wesleyanism to claim sinless perfection as a present possibility. But we must not let a reactionary posture blind us to the biblical hope that God Himself will "sanctify [us] *wholly*" and keep our "spirit and soul and body . . . sound and blameless at the coming of our Lord Jesus Christ" (1 Thess. 5:23). Although we are already free from domination by sin (1 John 3:4-10), we will continue to be liable to acts of sin (1:5-10) until our earthly journey is complete (3:1-3). The last chapter of this study will summarize how sanctification is deepened and enriched until its final goal is reached in the consummation of our salvation.

Bibliography

Hulme, William E. *The Dynamics of Sanctification.* Minneapolis: Augsburg, 1966. 194 pages.

14

Consummation

In this section of our study, I have stressed repeatedly that the "working out" of one's own salvation (Phil. 2:12) relates directly to the whole of Christian discipleship. However, I need not describe the connection in detail because several volumes in the "Layman's Library of Christian Doctrine" treat that theme, especially volume 11 on "Life in the Spirit." Instead, this final chapter of Part IV will show how our experience of God's salvation comes to an effective climax. This sense of fulfillment has many facets, several of which will be discussed elsewhere in this series, but three may be singled out for treatment here because they are so integral to the process which we have traced to this point.

Assurance

All of us know Christians whose spirit is one of hesitation, uncertainty, or confusion regarding the reality of their salvation. Perhaps they are baffled by the complexity of an adulthood which seems unrelated to the simplicity of a childhood profession of faith. Or the thrill of a dramatic conversion experience may have worn off, only to be replaced by the tedium of church responsibilities that offer little excitement. Again, their lives may have been lashed by physical illness, financial disaster, or domestic strife which their faith seemed powerless to prevent. Whatever the circumstances, many who view themselves as Christian have not yet claimed that unshakable confidence regarding the validity of their salvation experience which is promised by the New Testament to every believer.

The Promise of Assurance

No book is more realistic than the Bible regarding the doubts that can assail even the most sincere believer. After all, the early church was a pitifully small movement, harassed on every hand by enemies and sometimes hounded by actual persecution. As chapter after chapter in 1 Corinthians makes clear, numbered in the Christian fellowship were those who sinned so scandalously that it called into question the credibility of their claim to be saved. And yet the dominant mood was one of abounding assurance that, despite all of the believers' perplexities and imperfections, the God who had begun a good work in them would bring it to completion (Phil. 1:6).

Look for a moment at how this overwhelming sense of certainty was expressed. From the outset of the Christian life, confidence was contagious as the gospel came to new believers "in power and in the Holy Spirit and *with full conviction*" (1 Thess. 1:5). But as the Christian life developed, it became necessary to "exhort one another every day" so that the spiritually immature would "hold [their] *first confidence* firm to the *end*" (Heb. 3:14). This they could do if they would show "earnestness in realizing the *full assurance* of hope" (6:11) and would draw near to God "with a true heart in *full assurance* of faith" (10:22, author's italics throughout; compare Eph. 3:12). Ultimately, the "confidence" bestowed by salvation was "through Christ toward God" (2 Cor. 3:4) but, because all believers could possess it (2 Cor. 10:7), this meant that, in a secondary sense, they could also have "perfect confidence" in each other (2 Cor. 7:16; compare Gal. 5:10; 2 Thess. 3:4).

Colossians 2:1-6 is a typical pastoral passage in which we can glimpse the great strivings of the apostle Paul on behalf of the Laodicean converts (v. 1) lest they be "delude[d] with beguiling speech" (v. 4). Again and again he sought to stabilize their faith "that their hearts may be encouraged as they are knit together in love, to have all of the riches of *assured* understanding" (v. 2), so that he could rejoice to see the "good order" and the "firmness" of their faith in Christ (v. 5). The concluding exhortation underscored Paul's constant concern that they live in Christ, "*rooted* and *built up* in him and *established* in the faith" (v. 6). Think of how frequently Paul modeled this resolute certitude by prefacing one of his pronoucements with a phrase such as "I am *sure*" (for example, Rom. 8:38; Phil. 1:6; 2 Tim. 1:12).

All of these texts clearly teach that we may not only be saved and know it but also, as our salvation progresses and matures, may gain an ever-deeper confirmation of its authenticity. Such assurance is not automatic, however, else there would be no need for the repeated plea to "be the more zealous to *confirm* your call and election" (2 Pet. 1:10). But a sense of security is available to every Christian, as experience repeatedly testifies.

The Problem of Assurance

The breakthrough to what Fanny Crosby called "blessed assurance" is not without its difficulties, however. For a fine line exists between assurance and arrogance, confidence and complacency, persuasion and presumption. Unfortunately, we see too many examples of those at either extreme and not enough of those who strike a delicate balance in the center. On the one hand, the timid, tentative types are so wishy-washy about their faith that they exude no confidence in its reality. On the other hand, the aggressive, authoritarian types are so dogmatic about their faith that they have no room for unresolved questions. Stated simply a lot of Christians seem to have either too little or too much assurance!

When these two extremes meet, there is great danger of distorting the experience of salvation. For example, an over-confident preacher may press hearers to decide whether they are absolutely sure of their salvation. If there is any hesitation in giving an affirmative answer, underconfident hearers may conclude that they should profess faith and be baptized all over again in the hope of gaining a certainty which was previously lacking. The program with this approach is twofold. First, the New Testament teaches that assurance may come at the outset, but a deeper assurance may come at a subsequent stage in the salvation process. The hesitation is not necessarily an indication that one is still unsaved. Second, assurance comes not from baptism, or even from rebaptism, but from a dynamic process of spiritual development which may cover many years. Even though assurance is within the salvation experience from the beginning, it ripens as the result of mature growth in Christ.

Does this mean, then, that assurance is something we must earn by a lifetime of religious works? No, its achievement is better understood as two sides of the same coin, one side a gift and the other side a task. To illustrate: Climbing a mountain provides panoramic vistas unavailable in the valley. The mountain itself is a gift. It was here long before we arrived and will be here long after we are gone. All of our effort cannot even begin to build a mountain peak, and yet the only effective way to respond to its availability is by climbing the mountain ourselves. After hours of toil, we may reach the summit, yet the peak was there all the time waiting to be claimed. In like manner, assurance is "there" at the summit of the salvation experience, a gift of God to be claimed by those willing "to scale the utmost height And catch a gleam of glory bright."

The Proof of Assurance

If we ask how such assurance may be claimed, the answer of Scripture is that our confidence lies not in ourselves but in God. "By this we shall *know* that we are of the truth, and *reassure* our hearts before him whenever our hearts condemn us, for *God is greater* than our hearts, and he knows everything" (1 John 3:19-20). In other words, the basis of our assurance is objective rather than subjective, divine rather than human. We are confident *in the Lord* (Phil. 1:14; 2 Thess. 3:4; 1 Tim. 3:13; 1 Pet. 1:21; 1 John 5:14). Our task is not to boost our sagging spirits with psychological self-assurance but to examine ourselves, to test ourselves to determine if we are holding fast to the certainties offered us by God (2 Cor. 13:5). Fortunately, an entire book of the Bible, 1 John, is devoted to clarifying the ways in which "[we] may *know* that [we] have eternal life" (5:13). Three tests are prescribed for our self-examination (3:21-23, author's italics).

The Test of Belief.—First John recognizes with sober realism that our world is filled with deception and falsehood. No truth is denied more vigorously by the world than that Jesus of Nazareth is actually the Christ of messianic hope (2:22). Absurd, cry some, that an obscure Jewish carpenter should be the unique son of God the Father! Such attacks are attributed to the "many antichrists" (v. 18) who have come to corrupt the church with their lies (v. 22). But if we confess both the Son and the Father (v. 23) by letting the saving gospel "abide" in our hearts, then we have both the Son and the Father and "abide" in them continually (v. 24). This belief centers on the incarnation in a threefold confession (a) "that Jesus Christ has come in the flesh" (4:2), (b) to be "the Savior of the world" (v. 14), (c) because of God's love for us (v. 16). Such faith furnishes us with victorious assurance because it "overcomes the world" (5:4).

The Test of Obedience.—The reason belief is so powerful in 1 John is that it refers, not to the acceptance of a proposition, but to having and abiding in God the Father, Son, and Holy Spirit (4:13-15). But if we are energized and sustained by the divine life, we will also "keep his commandments," and by this righteous conduct "we may be sure that we know him" (2:3). There is simply no way to be "born" of a righteous person without being righteous ourselves (v. 29)! Such is the law of spiritual heredity (3:7-10). Sin saps our sense of confidence that we are saved. If we capitulate again and again to temptation, our assurance is eroded. But if we get serious about cleansing sin from our lives and consistently rebuff its enticements, we prove afresh that the saving power of God is really at work in our lives (3:24).

The Test of Fellowship.—Faith means believing in the God who loved us enough to send His Son in the flesh to save us and abide with us. But 1 John goes on to insist, "If God so loved us, we also ought to love one another. . . . if we love one another, God abides in us and his love is *perfected* in us" (4:11-12). When divine love expresses itself in human relationships (that is, when we love one another with God's love), the result is fellowship. This bonding experience provides reinforcement to individual Christians by rooting their lives in a community dedicated to nourishing the wellsprings of faith. Notice how 1 John interrelates the three tests: "I am writing you a *new commandment* [the test of obedience], which is *true in him* [the test of belief]. . . . He who *loves his brother* [the test of fellowship] abides in the light, and in it there is no cause for stumbling" (2:8,10, author's italics).

Perseverance

One reason seeking a sense of "blessed assurance" is so important is that those who lack such confidence may come to fear the loss of salvation itself. After all, Christianity differed from both Judaism and Hellenism by claiming that a person could be saved in a world where nothing seemed to change. In other religions, salvation was promised in a future age when everything would be transformed, but the gospel dared to offer salvation here and now in the midst of sin and death. In other words, most religions envisioned salvation as being supported by the *best* possible environment, whereas the Christian faith insisted that salvation could begin in the *worst* possible environment. Obviously it was one thing to enjoy salvation in paradise, but quite another thing to hold on to it in Corinth! How could this be done?

The Divine Faithfulness

Since God graciously decided to make salvation available "ahead of time," as it were, that same God will see that what was inaugurated in weakness will be consummated in strength. First Peter explains that our salvation is like an inheritance being "kept in heaven" for us until we are able to claim it (1:4). Meanwhile, we live as those "who *by God's power* are guarded through faith for a salvation ready to be revealed in the last time" (v. 5). The decision of God to save us over a lifetime is rooted in God's determination to see the entire process through to its completion. Again and again the New Testament bears witness to such a conviction in the recurring refrain: *"God is faithful"* (1 Cor. 1:9; 10:13; 2 Cor. 1:18; see 1 Thess. 5:24).

This affirmation is based not only on the experience of the believer but also on an unshakable assumption regarding the character of God. Note the sure saying (2 Tim. 2:11): "If we are faithless, he remains faithful—for *he cannot deny himself*" (v. 13). This truth suggests that God's very nature is reliable, steadfast, even tenacious in the accomplishment of His purposes. God is not fickle, offering salvation at one time and withdrawing it at another. His willingness to launch the salvation process in a human life is, in itself, a pledge, a bond, a guarantee that He will honor His word given us in the gospel (compare Eph. 1:13-14; 4:30). This divine dependability does not mean, however, that we are relieved of any responsibility to be faithful to the end: "God's firm foundation stands, bearing this seal: The Lord knows those who are his, *and* Let every one who names the name of the Lord depart from iniquity" (2 Tim. 2:19).

A few days before I wrote these pages, my wife and I visited a new grandson for the first time. Since he was only three months old, Andrew could not walk or talk or show any sign that he recognized his proud grandparents. Yet we did not reject him because he had not been born as a fully grown adult. For years to come, that little fellow is going to be a heavy responsibility to his parents. They will get up many times in the night to change and feed him. By slow degree they will have to teach him every skill needed to live on his own. And yet they made that commitment to his care even before he was born! If parents are to be responsible, the decision to have a baby must be a decision to do whatever it takes to help that baby reach full maturity.

Just so, God begets us as spiritual babes (1 Pet. 1:23) and provides us with "pure spiritual milk" by which we "may grow up to salvation" (2:2) and be ready for "solid food" (Heb. 5:12-14). During this long period of growing to maturity we may cry out many times in dark nights of doubt and fear, but our Heavenly Father never fails to come to the rescue. To say that "God is faithful" does not mean that He will pamper us or indulge us or spoil us. Rather, it means that He will patiently pay the price to guide us to spiritual adulthood, however long that may take.

Just as a child never outgrows the love of caring parents, so we can always count on the devotion of God to our ultimate well-being.

The Intolerable Compliment

The unwearying support from our divine parent does not exempt us, however, from earthly threats to our salvation. If anything, we experience twice the harassment inflicted on others because we receive not only a full share of the sufferings common to all humanity but also resistance to the stand which we take for the cause of Christ. Evil has little reason to retaliate against the spiritually uncommitted, thus it can focus its attack on those who pose the greatest threat to its power. In the early church, persecution became so fierce that it sometimes led to martyrdom, which is still a danger today in militantly athcistic countries. For most of us, however, the pressure is more subtle but the threat no less real from such insidious temptations as secularism, materialism and hedonism (pleasure as the goal of life). Satan works twice as hard to seduce believers since success with them has the double payoff of corrupting their own commitment and compromising their witness to others.

Against this background of a deliberate conspiracy to undermine God's salvation we must deal soberly and resolutely with the peril of backsliding or falling away as described in the Bible. Far from being a minor theme, this is a dominant concern running throughout Scripture. The Old Testament is full of prophetic condemnations of Israel because the people had forsaken their covenant with God (for example, Deut. 32; Ps. 78; Jer. 3). The interbiblical writings warn increasingly of a great apostasy to take place at the end of the age (for example, Dead Sea Scrolls, Zadokite Document). The New Testament spares nothing in describing the fate of such failures as Judas (Acts 1:25), Ananias and Sapphira (5:1-11), Simon Magus (8:9-24), Demas (2 Tim. 4:10), and Hymenaeus and Alexander (1 Tim. 1:19-20). In the face of such relentless temptation, how may a believer persevere to the end?

A Strategy of Endurance

The New Testament strategy of endurance, generally speaking, falls into three categories: (1) Beware of professed faith that does not persevere. It is relatively easy to make an impulsive response to the gospel that is sincere but without depth. Lacking roots, such a superficial commitment soon withers and dies (Mark 4:16-17) whereas a genuine faith has within it the dynamic quality of continuous growth. (2) Heed the admonitions to be vigilant (1 Cor. 10:12). Someone has said that the greatest defense against sin consists in our ability to be shocked by it. Even the assurance of salvation should not produce an attitude of overconfidence which makes us vulnerable to the seductive power of evil. (3) Finally, submit to the discipline of the Christian community. Rather than trying to go it alone, be open to the admonitions of the spiritually mature (Acts 20:31; Col. 3:16). There is shared strength in meeting together to exhort one another to continue in the faith (Acts 11:23; 14:22; 1 Thess. 5:14; Heb. 3:12-13).

When one takes time to study every warning, admonition, and exhortation in the New Testament, he receives the strong impression that the early Christians sought to live in a perpetual state of preparedness. In times of possible danger, our military forces are put "on alert," but the first disciples endeavored to maintain a constant watchfulness (Mark 13:37) because they knew that their spiritual enemies could strike at any moment. Today we often speculate on various theories of "once saved—always saved" within the safe confines of a powerful Christian establishment. But 1,900 years ago, the New Testament writers were not systematic theologians trying to explain all the sides of assurance and perseverance. Rather, acutely aware of just how vulnerable they were to attack, the embattled followers of Jesus lived in "combat readiness" for spiritual warfare (compare Eph. 6:10-20). If we would bring the same urgency to our engagement with evil, we would discover, as did they, that in Christ "we are more than conquerors" (Rom. 8:37).

Glorification

God in His faithfulness perseveres with us, and we in our faithfulness persevere with Him, resulting in a salvation that does indeed "endure to the end." What else is there about our salvation experience that is yet to come? Stated differently, if perseverance involves such a fierce battle with temptation, is its climax in the world beyond worth all of our struggle while here on earth? To answer such questions, we must first define salvation in its future dimension. According to the New Testament, the content of that final consummation may be expressed by one word: *glory*. As Paul put it in Romans 5:1-2, the whole salvation process, which includes such things as being "justified by faith," having "peace with God," and obtaining "access to [His] grace in which we stand," has as its climax "our hope of sharing the *glory* of God" (v. 2). Or as he expressed it in Colossians 1:27, "Christ in you" (that is, salvation) is "the hope of *glory*."

To us, the word *glory* often suggests brightness or radiance, hence the idea that the saved will one day share God's glory might connote to some that in heaven we will be cleansed of all our sins and glisten like the sun. But in the Old Testament the word *glory* was based on a root meaning "weightiness" and in the New Testament on a root meaning "reputation." More precisely, therefore, God's glory is His "weighty reputation," what we might today call His prestige or His clout (see Isa. 42:8). For us to have a "hope of glory" means that we may rightly expect one day to share the significance of what it means for God to be God! All of us can imagine what it would be like in earthly experience to belong to a king's court or a president's cabinet: It would involve direct participation in the weighty affairs of state. Similarly, "to share the glory of God" means to be engaged with Him in the exercise of His deity (that is, to play a part in the governance of the universe)!

According to the Bible, this final stage in the salvation process represents the culmination of an agelong drama in two acts. The first part is a movement of God to mankind in which He gives His glory to us. The second part is a movement of believers to God in which we learn to give His glory back to Him. Let us examine each of these stages in turn.

The Glory Which God Gives to Christians

In the earliest part of the Old Testament, God's glory was associated with His awesomeness. It abode in a cloud on the mountaintop, often accompanied by thunder and lightning, and its appearance was like a devouring fire (Ex. 24:17). So unapproachable was the divine glory that people could not look upon it and live (33:18-23). But soon this elusive glory came to dwell among men, first at the tabernacle in the wilderness and then at the Temple in Jerusalem (40:34-35; 1 Kings 8:10-13). After Jerusalem was destroyed and the people exiled in Bablyon, later Old Testament and intertestamental Judaism came to realize that the glory of God could fill the earth, especially wherever God was present with people in His Word (Isa. 60:1-2).

This process of permeating ordinary life with the glory of God came to a climax in Jesus of Nazareth. Jesus' earthly ministry was glory incarnate (John 1:14; Heb. 1:3), especially His miracles (John 2:11), His transfiguration (Luke 9:32), His crucifixion (John 17:1), and His resurrection (Luke 24:26). After the exaltation of Christ on high, His followers were permitted to "behold the glory of the Lord" through His indwelling Spirit (2 Cor. 3:18). Furthermore, they could look forward to His triumphant return when "the glory of his Father" (Mark 8:38) would fill the universe and be acknowledged by all (Phil. 2:11). Notice that, over this long process, the glory that no one could see in the beginning would be seen by all in the end. The divine majesty that was once inaccessible even to Moses was now available to anyone who would have it. The terror of Sinai had come down from the mountaintop to dwell in the humblest heart.

The Glory Which Christians Give to God

This initial movement of glory from God to mankind was not intended to impress earthlings with the divine grandeur, as if God's purpose were somehow to dazzle His creatures into submission. Rather, God offered His glory to ordinary men and women because they were all created in His "image," with a heavenly "likeness" (Gen. 1:26), and therefore capable of sharing the dignity that belongs only to Him. Unfortunately, senseless rebellion had "darkened" their existence, causing them to seek "glory" in the things of earth (Rom. 1:20-23). The tragic consequence of such sin was that it caused everyone to "fall short of the glory of God" (3:23). But the glory that fallen humanity forfeited in its refusal to honor God, Jesus Christ came to restore. This He did, first by allowing the Father to fill His own life with divine glory (John 17:1); and, second, by giving God's glory to all who, through faith, would become one with Him and the Father (v. 22).

Salvation means, to use a beautiful phrase from Paul, being "conformed to the *image* of [God's] Son" (Rom. 8:29). But that Son "reflects the *glory* of God and bears the very stamp of his nature" (Heb. 1:3). Hence, there is no way to accept Christ into our lives without seeking to glorify God just as Christ did during His earthly ministry (John 17:4). Because we are one with Christ through faith, there is a sense in which we are "glorified" from the outset of the salvation process (Rom. 8:30). But because being "conformed to His image" takes a lifetime, there is another sense in which we are slowly "being changed into his likeness from one *degree of glory* to another" (2 Cor. 3:18). Only gradually do we learn to glorify God in our conduct (Matt. 5:16), for example, by the harmony of our loving relationships with other Christians (Rom. 15:5-7; 1 Cor. 10:31). There is no way to show forth the fullness of God's glory in this age of suffering (Rom. 8:18), but even the afflictions of the present moment prepare Christians for "an eternal weight of glory beyond all comparison" (2 Cor. 4:17). Ultimately, our "hope of glory" (Col. 1:27) is finally to share "the glory of God" (Rom. 5:2) as fully as Christ shares it for all eternity (John 17:24)!

This last word of the Bible on the subject of salvation is breathtaking, indeed, in its vision of the possibilities of life in Christ. The secular "human potential movement" of today does not come close to this soaring prospect of God glorifying man and of man glorifying God. For what salvation means is that the Christian God, unlike any other, wants to share His splendor, His responsibilities, and His privileges. Our God is not possessive—even of His privileges as God! Furthermore, it is with ordinary people like you and me that He is willing to share His status. Imagine: God believes in us enough to entrust us with the riches that belong only to Him as God (Col. 1:27a). In so much of the world today, human life is cheap, with millions perishing at the whim of a dictator. Even in the West, life is cheapened by cynicism and despair. Against every putdown of human potential, the Christian doctrine of salvation fairly shouts, "You can be *glorified* for you matter infinitely to God!"

Bibliography

Law, Robert. *The Tests of Life: A Study of the First Epistle of St. John*. Third edition. Edinburgh: T. & T. Clark, 1914. 442 pages.

Marshall, I. Howard. *Kept by the Power of God: A Study of Perseverance and Falling Away*. London: Epworth Press, 1969. 228 pages.

Ramm, Bernard. *Them He Glorified: A Systematic Study of the Doctrine of Glorification*. Grand Rapids: Wm. B. Eerdmans Publishing Company, 1963. 148 pages.

Scripture Index

154   The Christian Experience of Salvation